Mandala

COLORING BOOK FOR MEDITATION

Pure Adults Relaxation with these Anti-Stress Relieving Designs

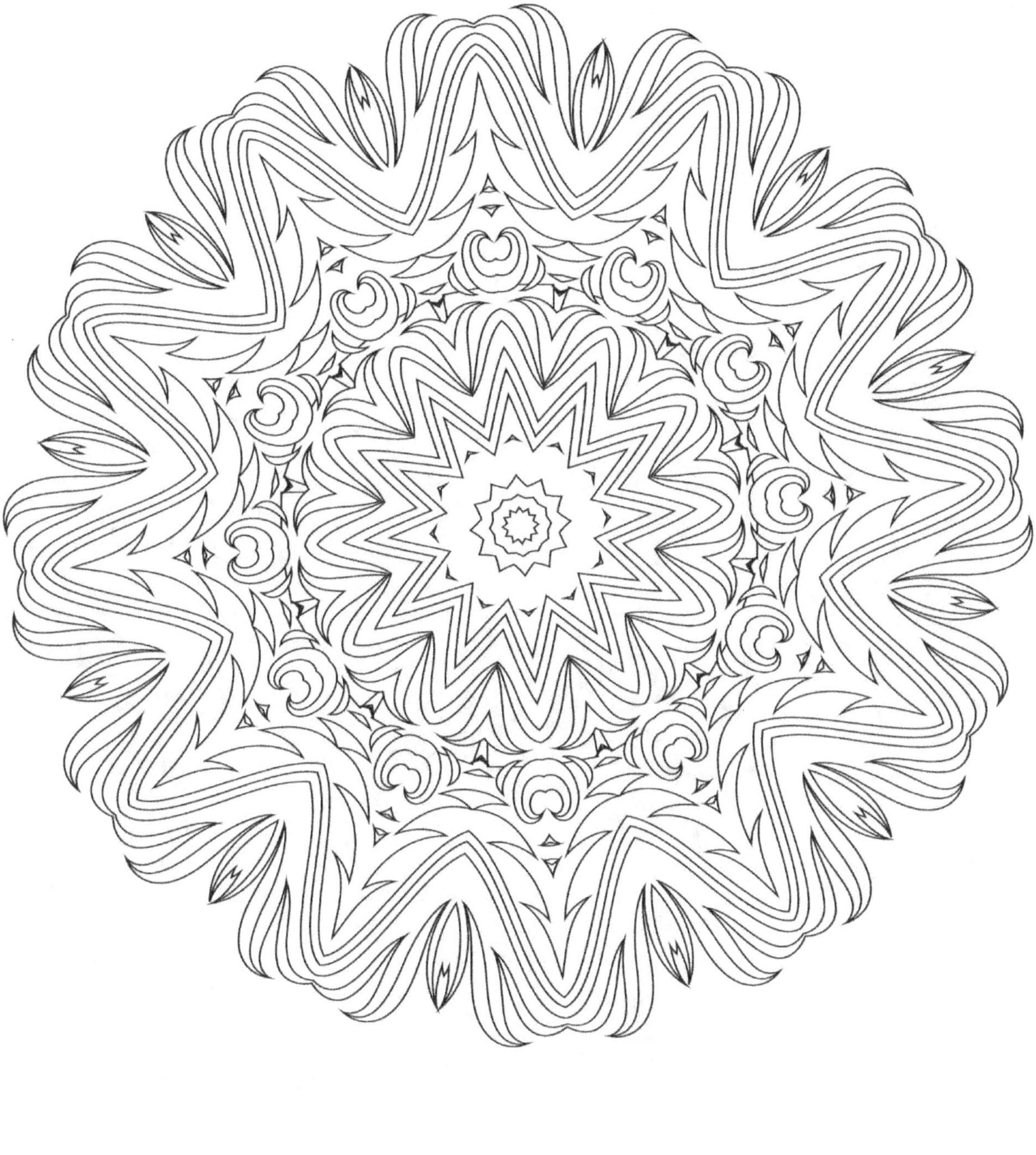

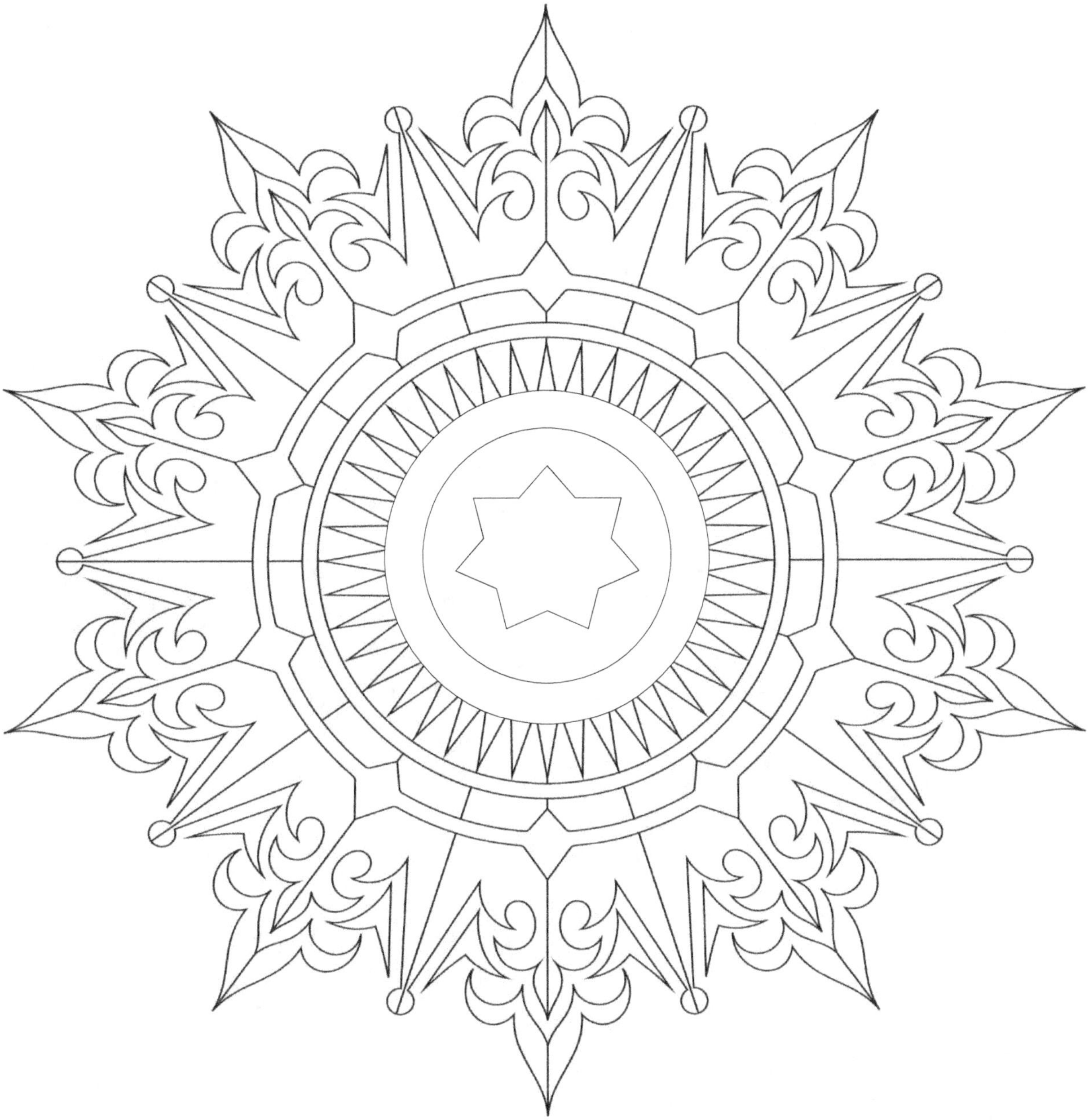

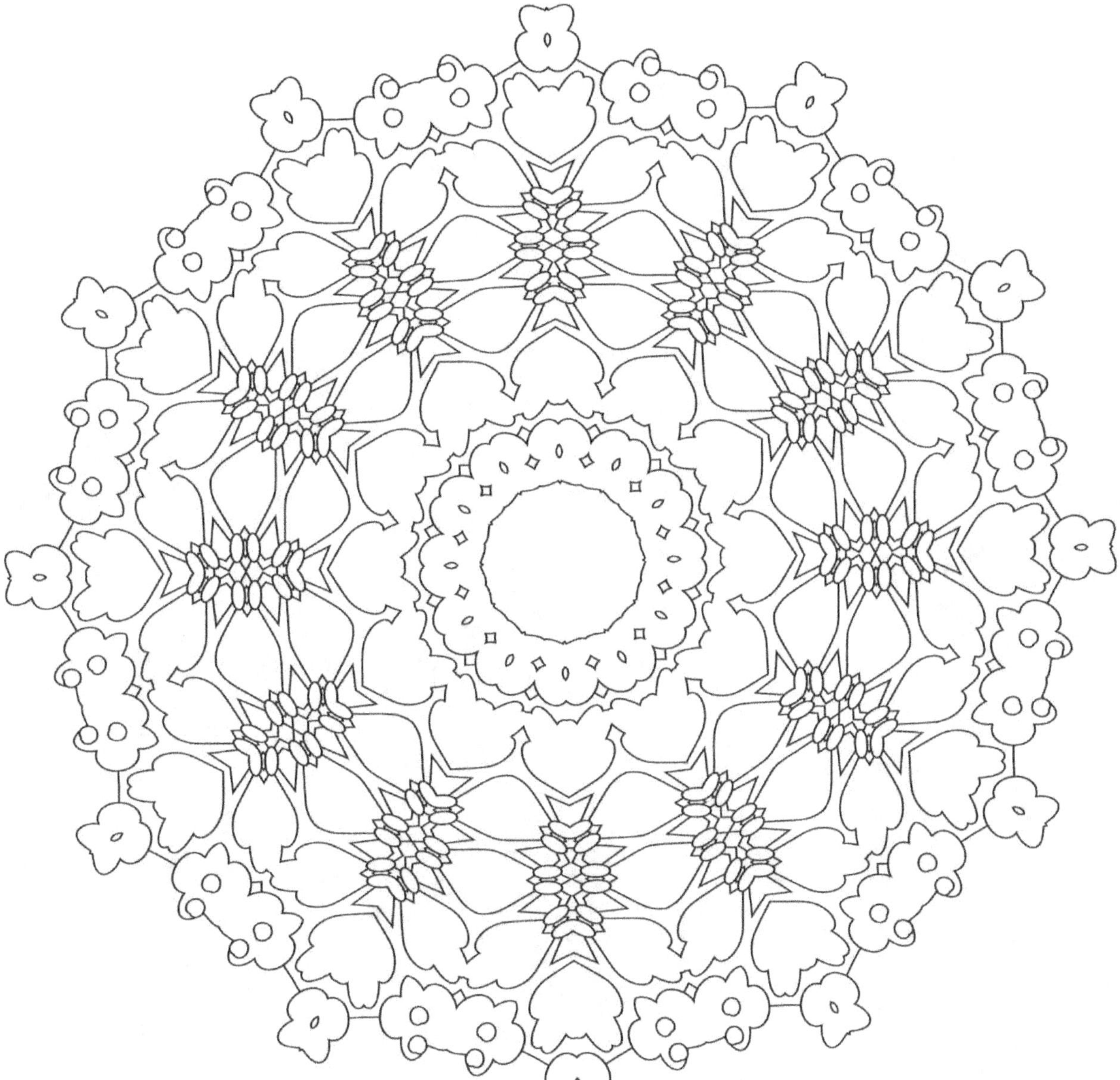

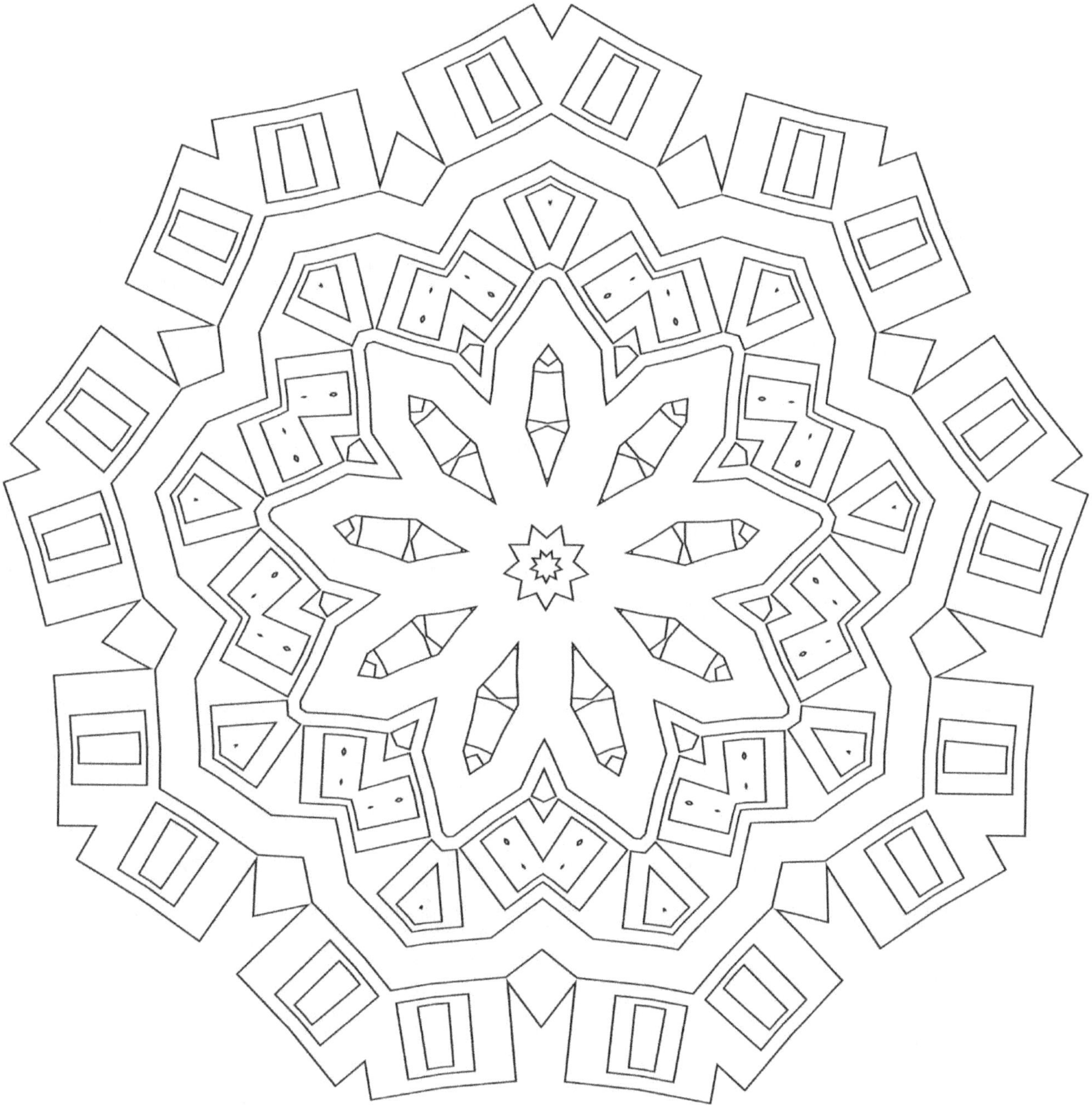

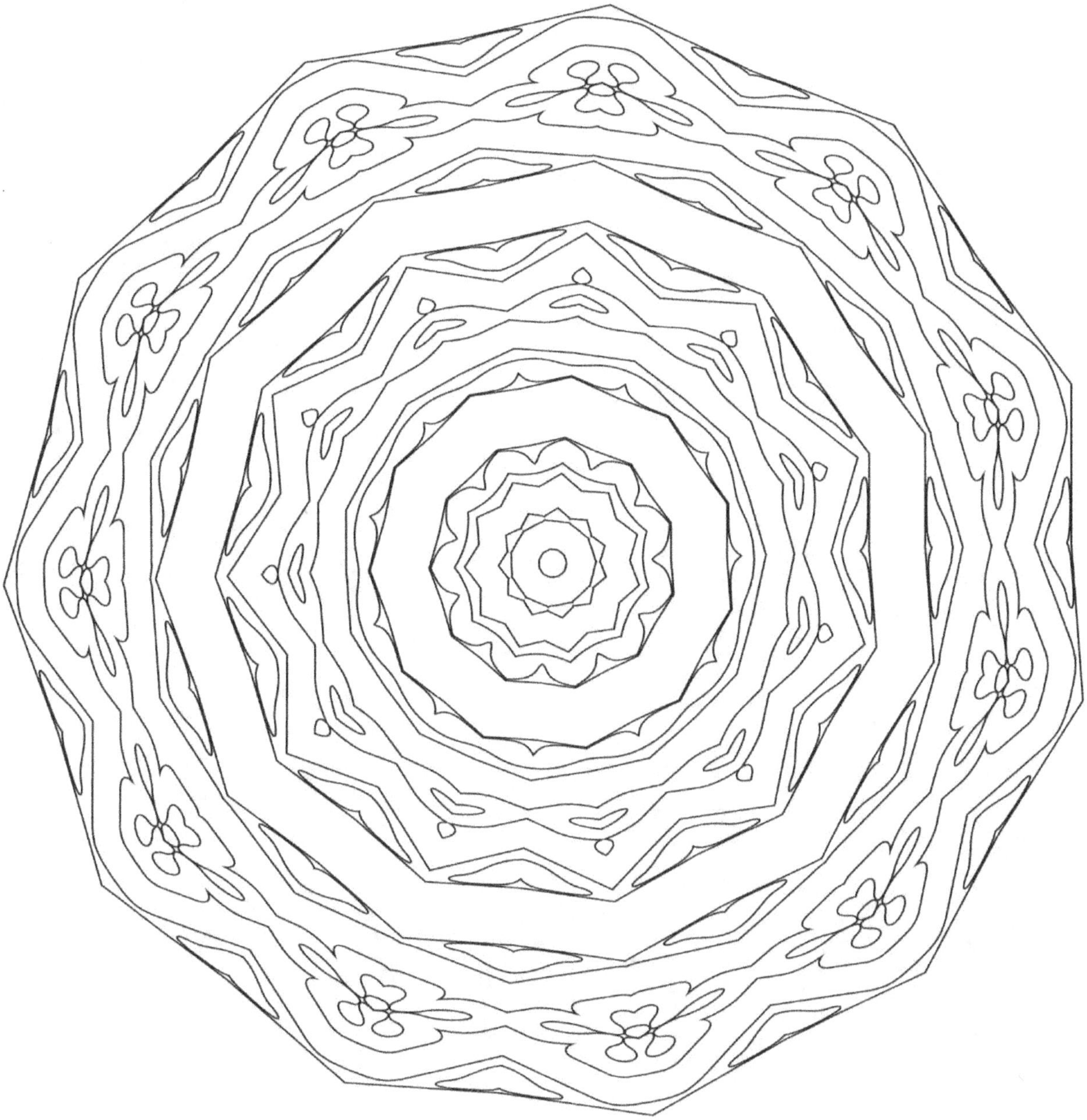

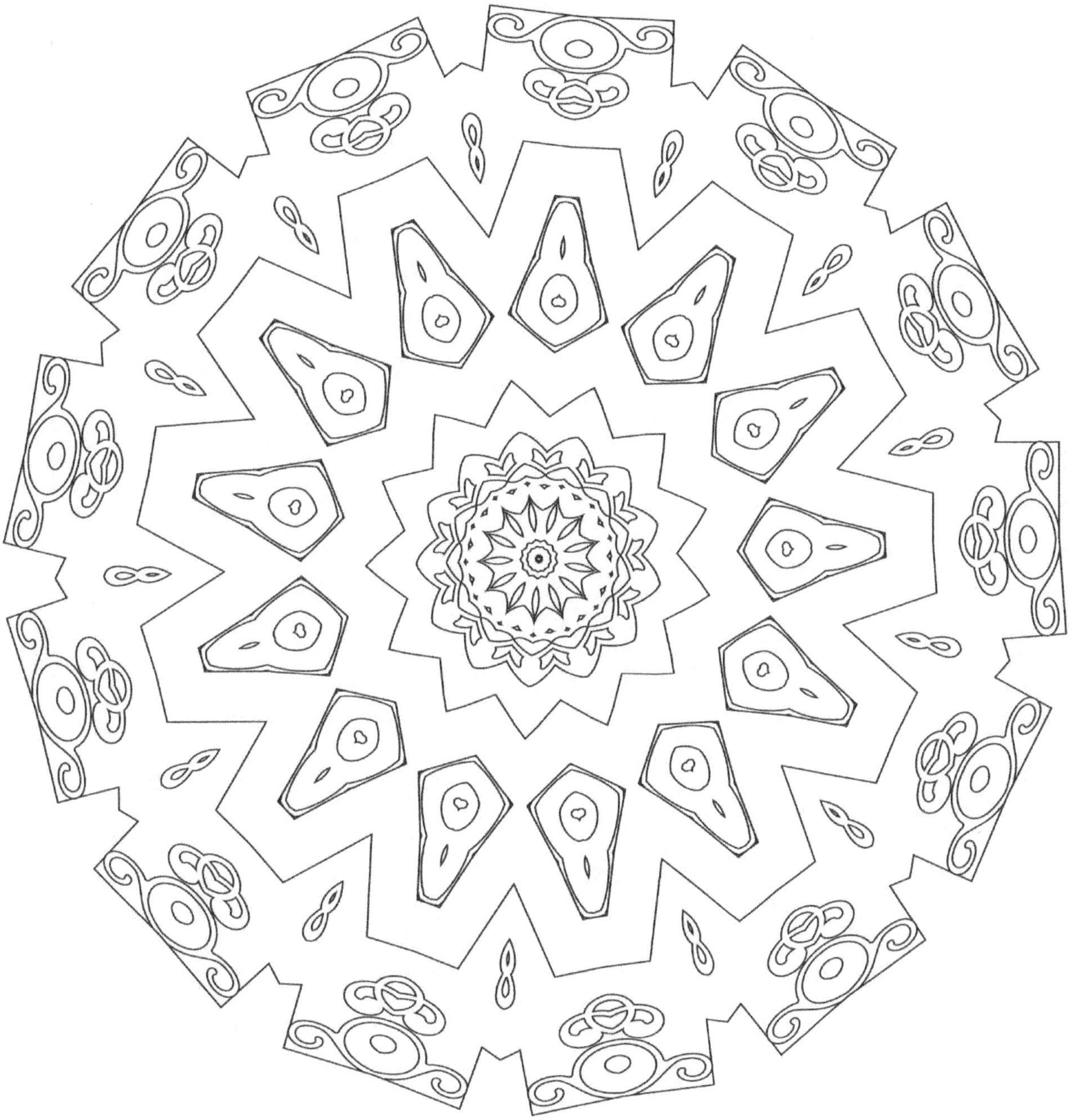

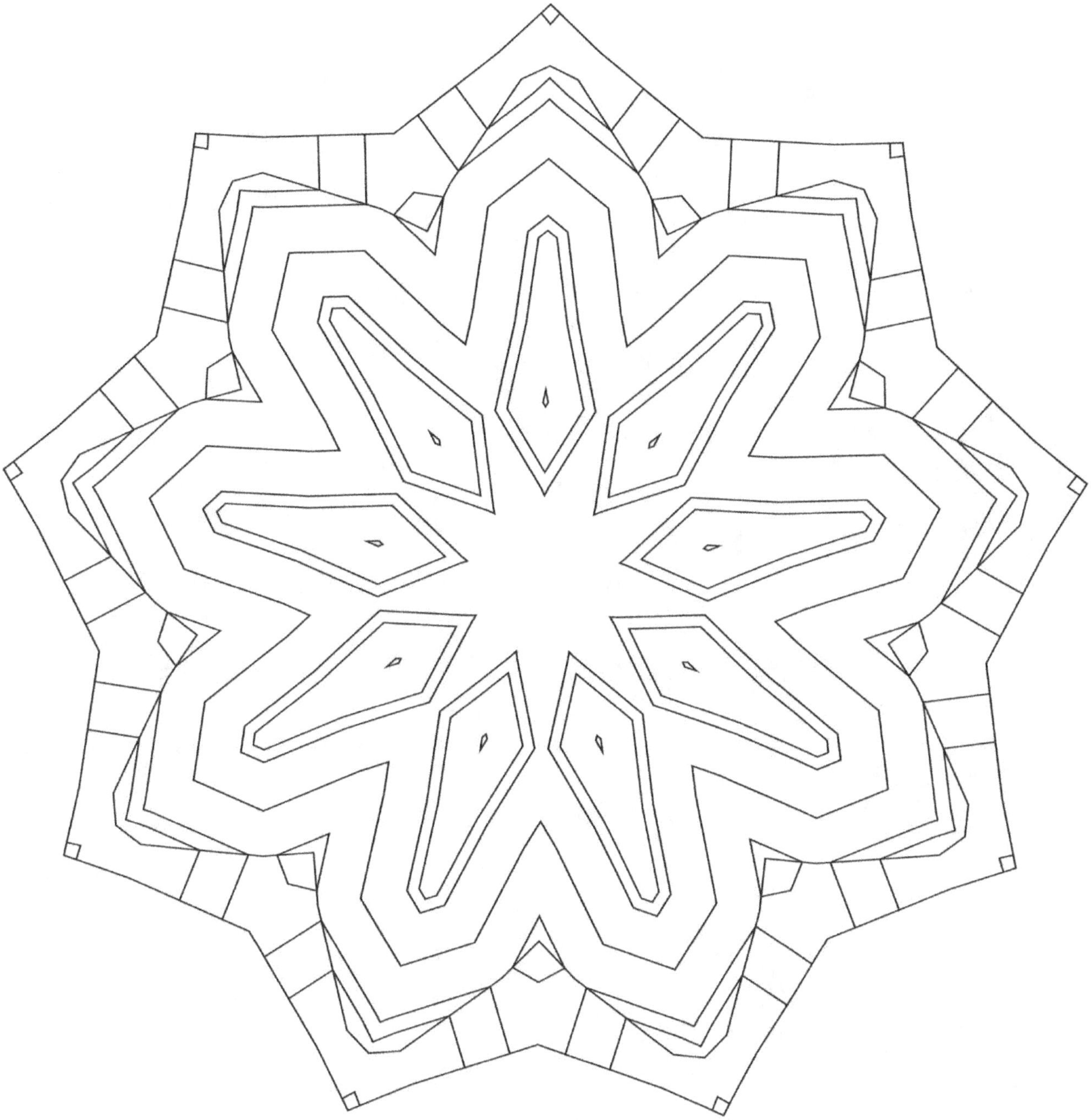

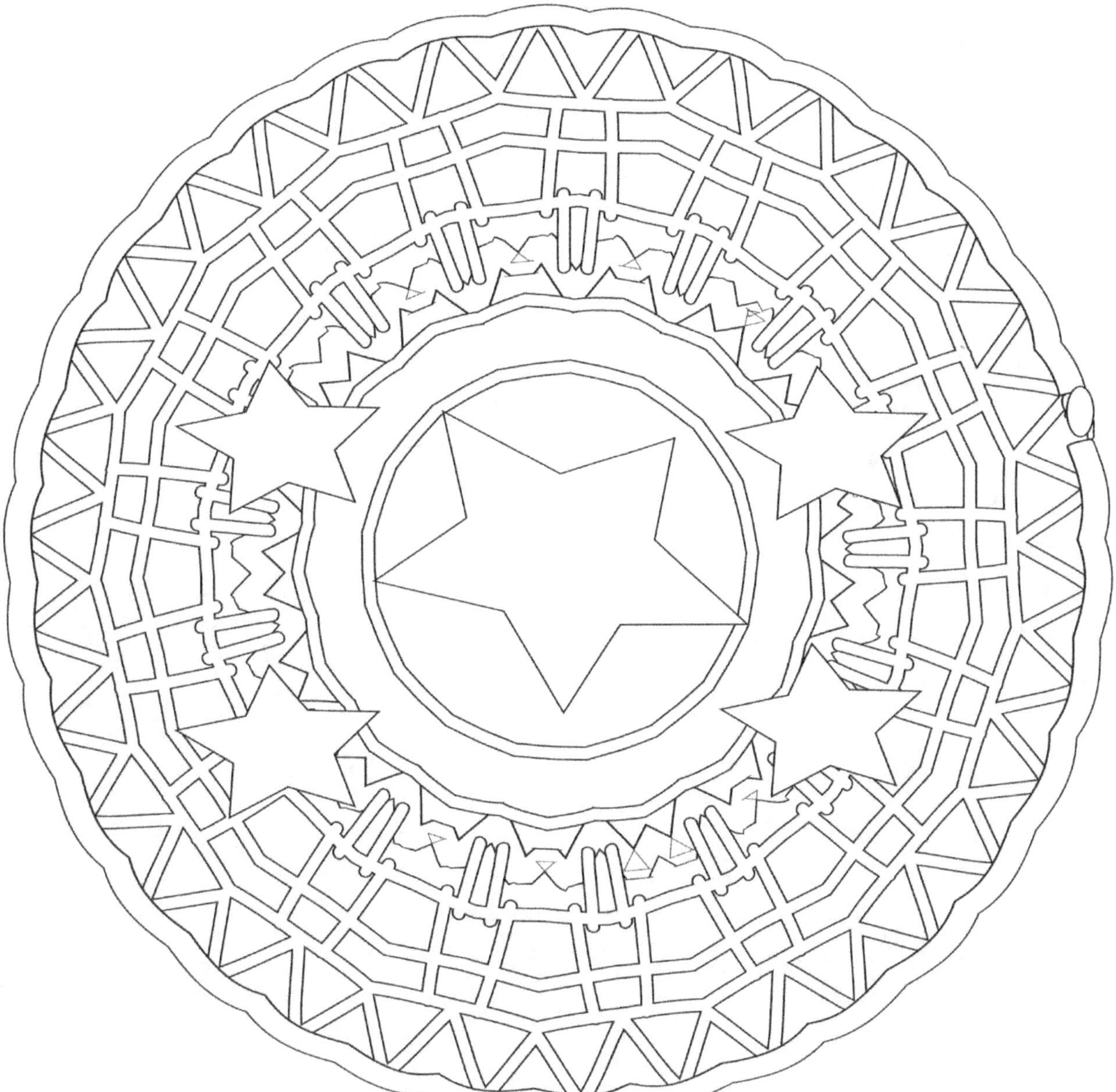

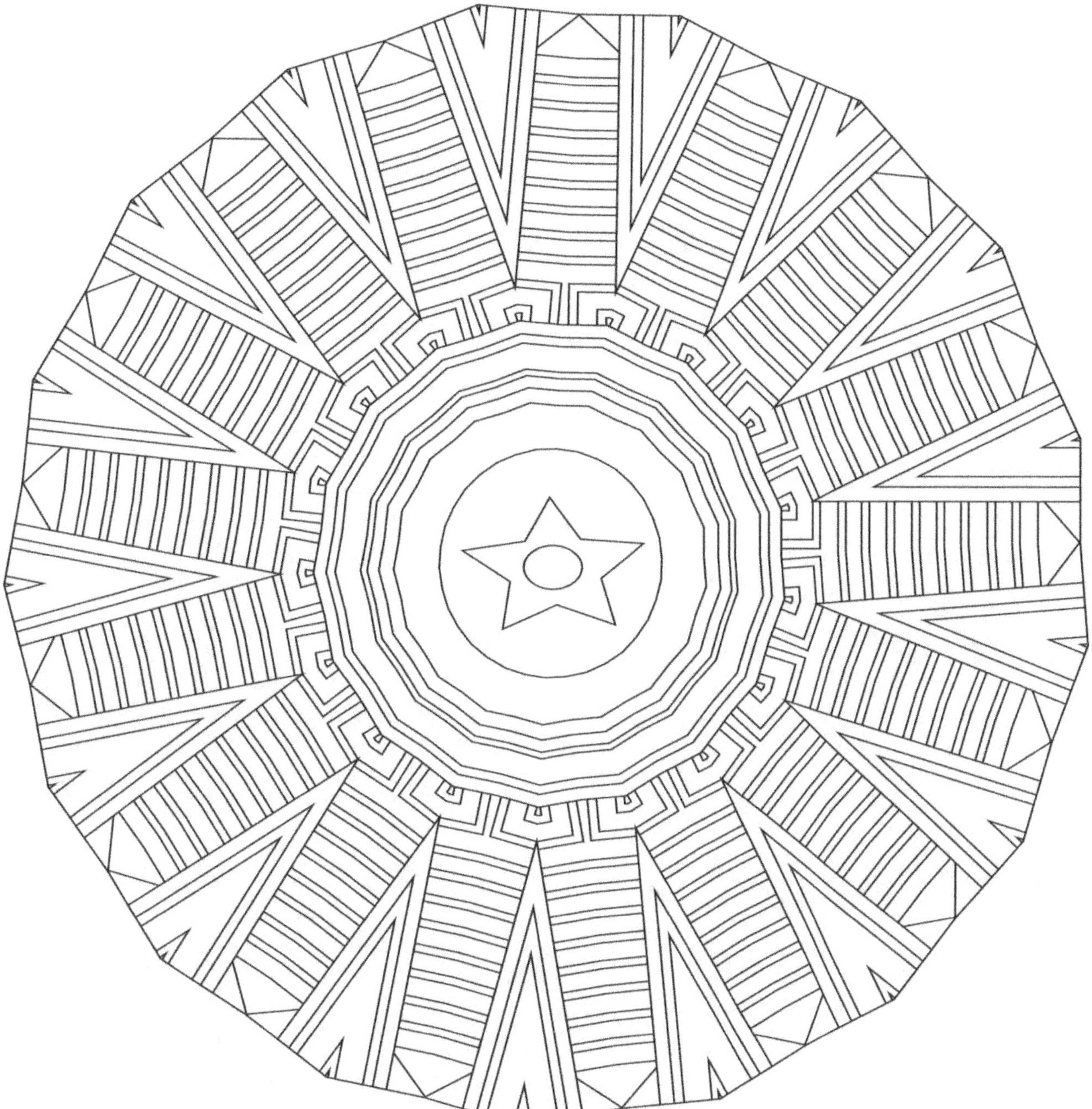

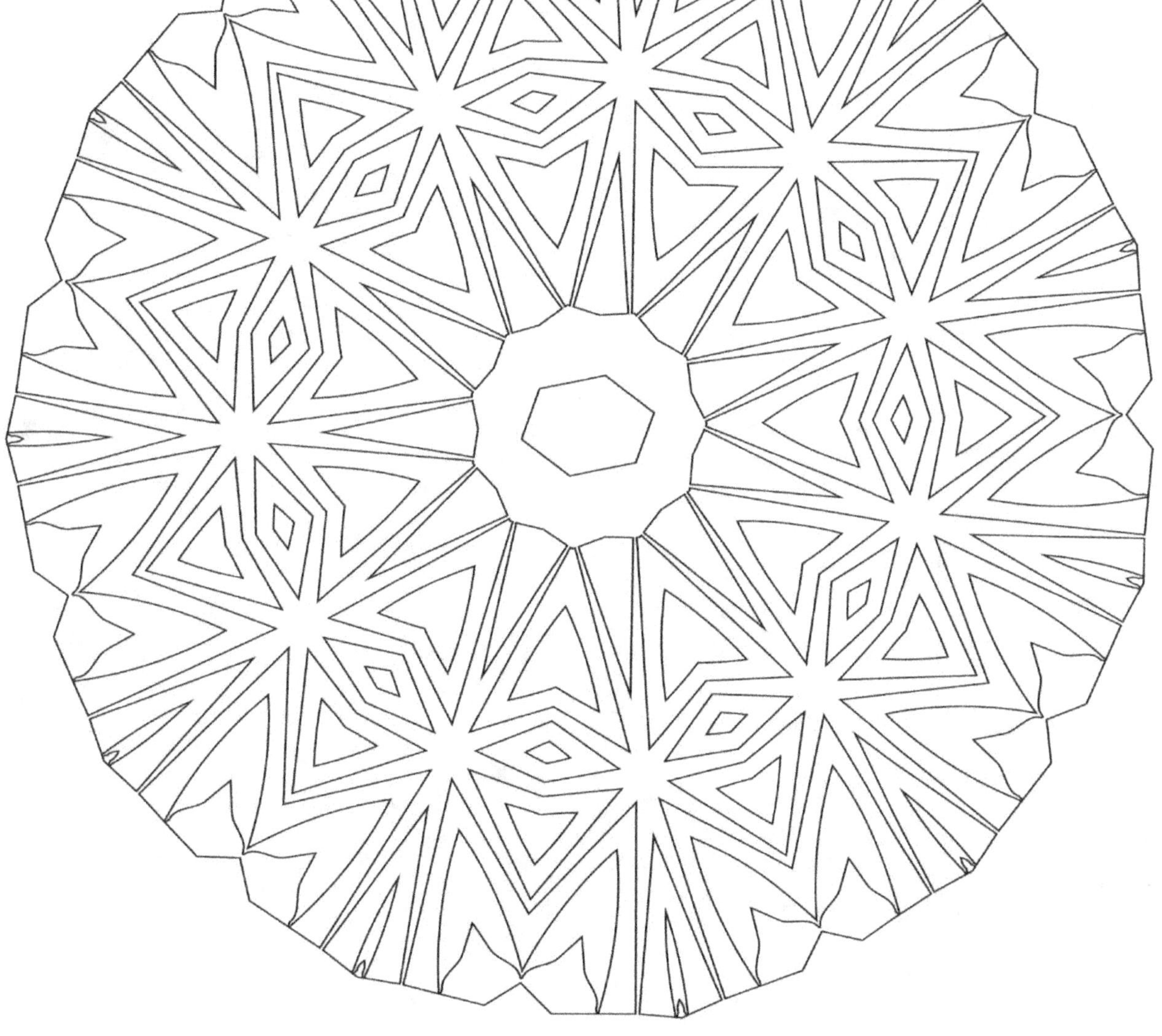

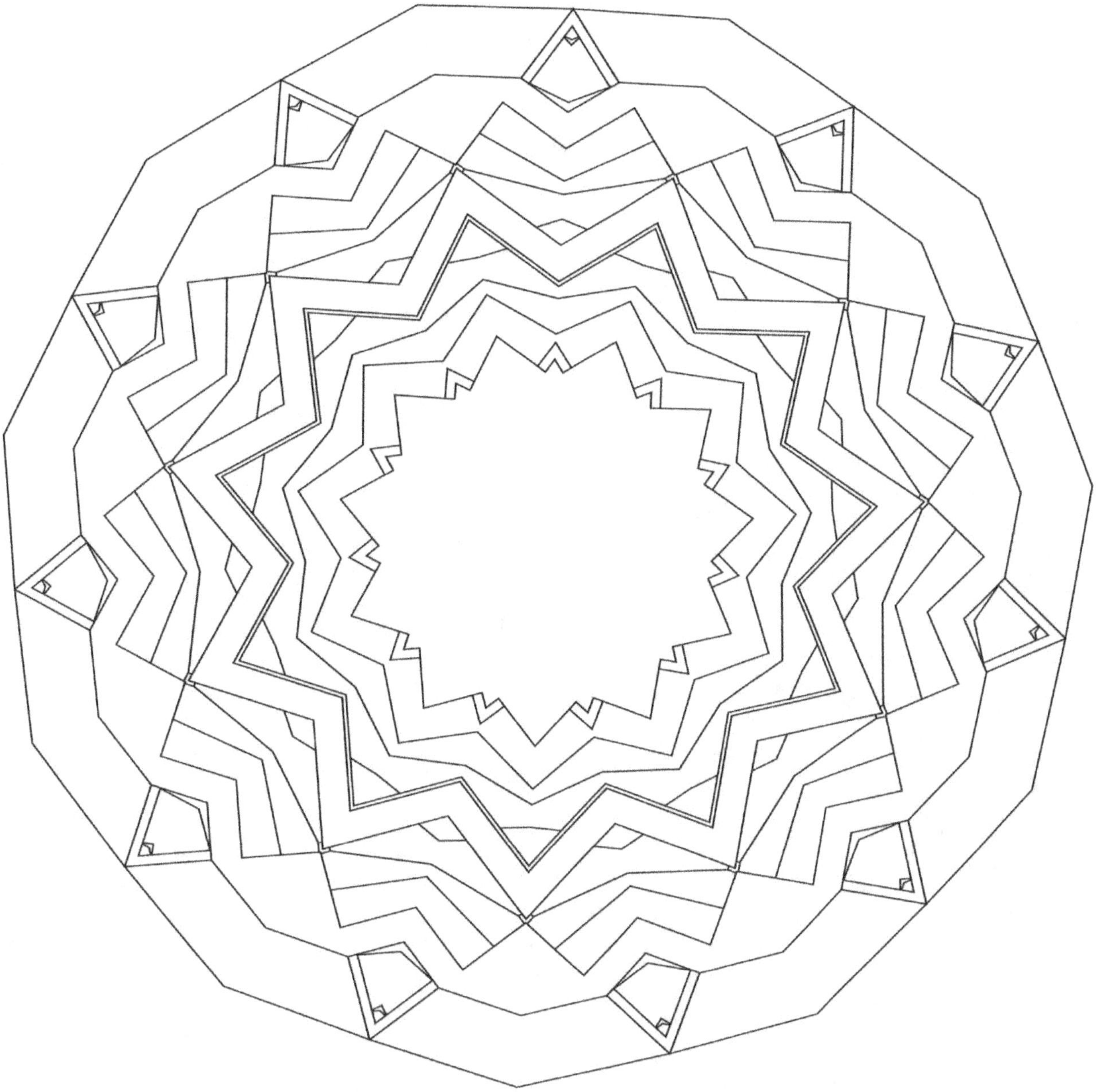

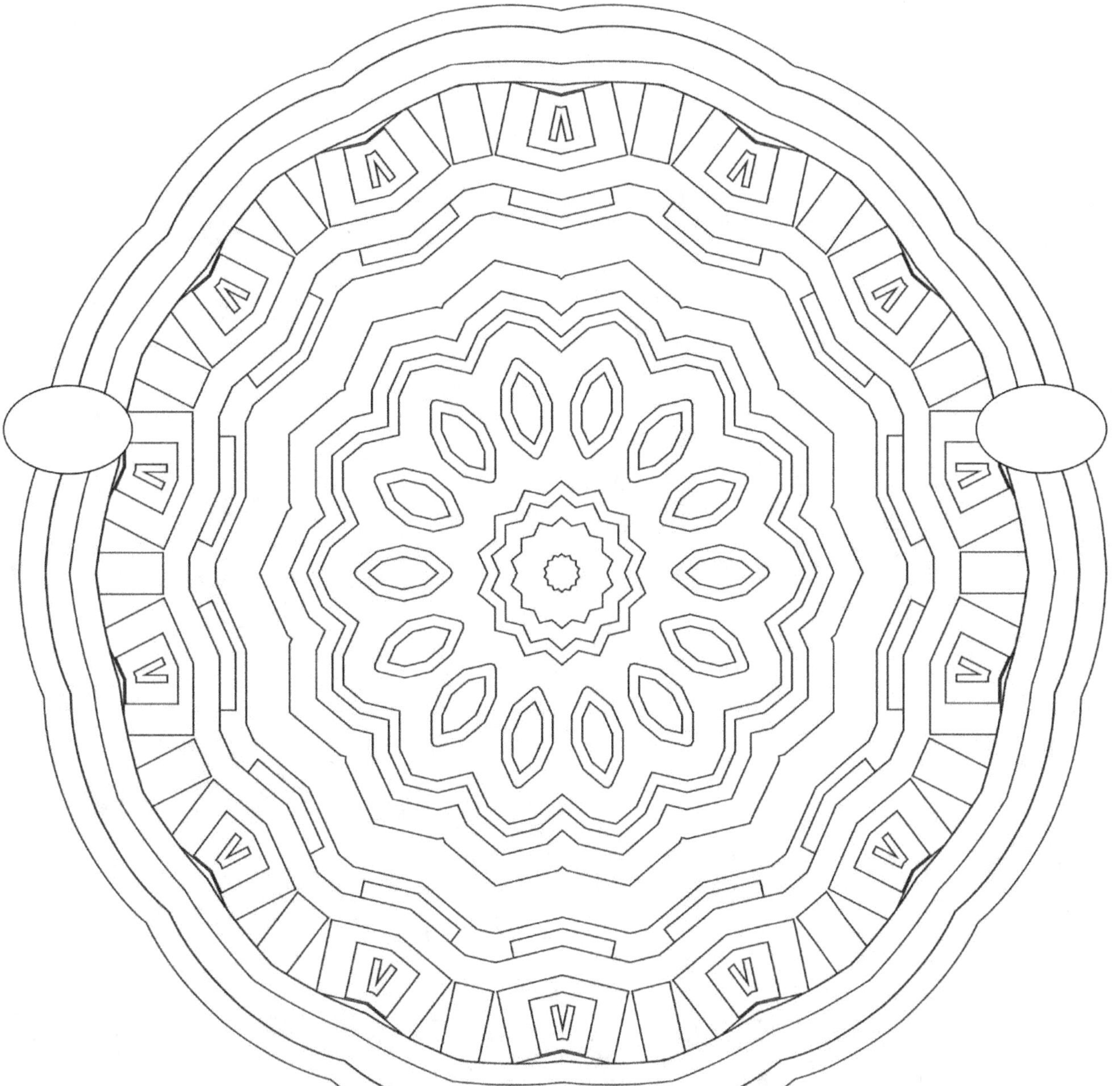

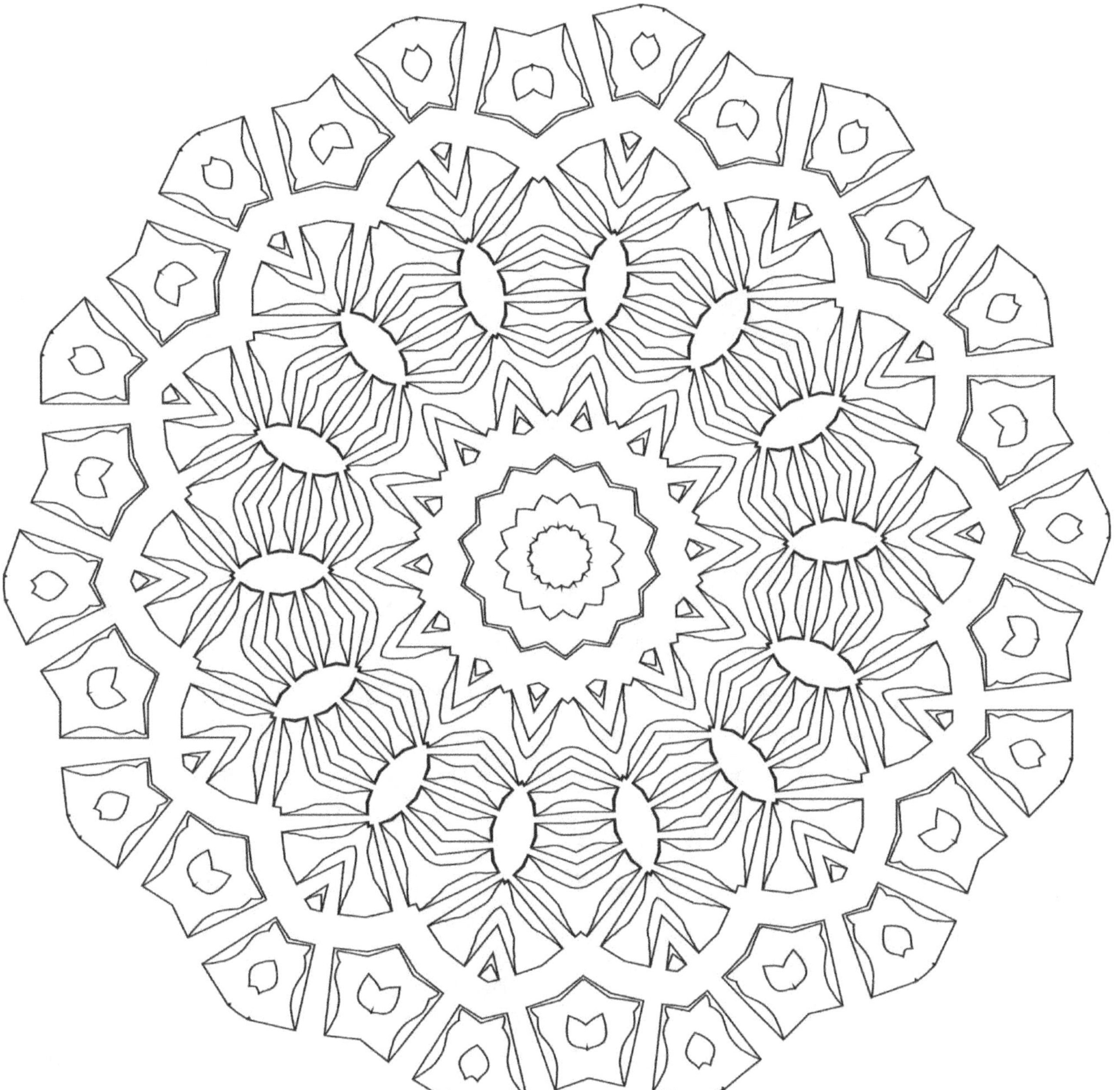

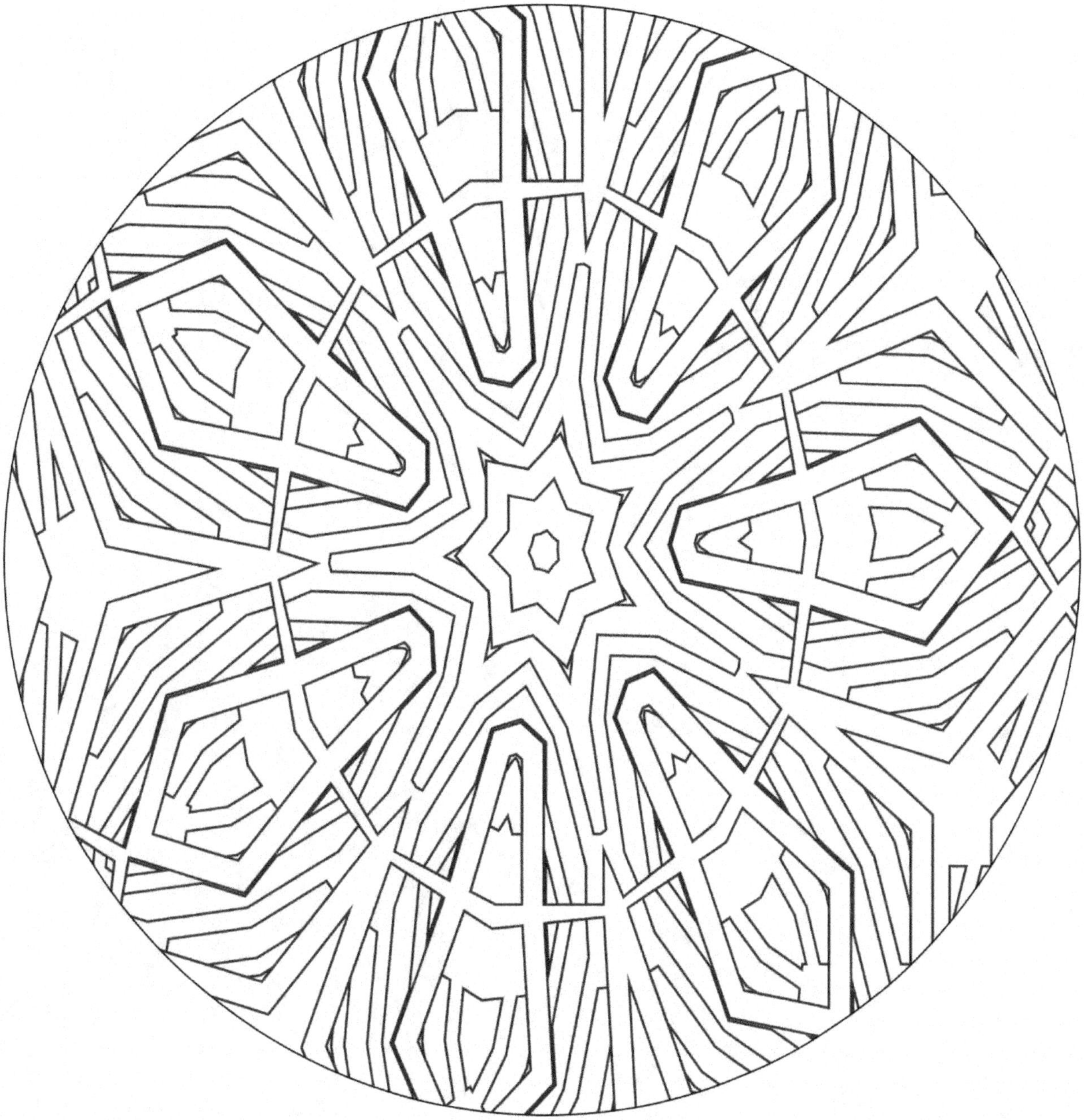

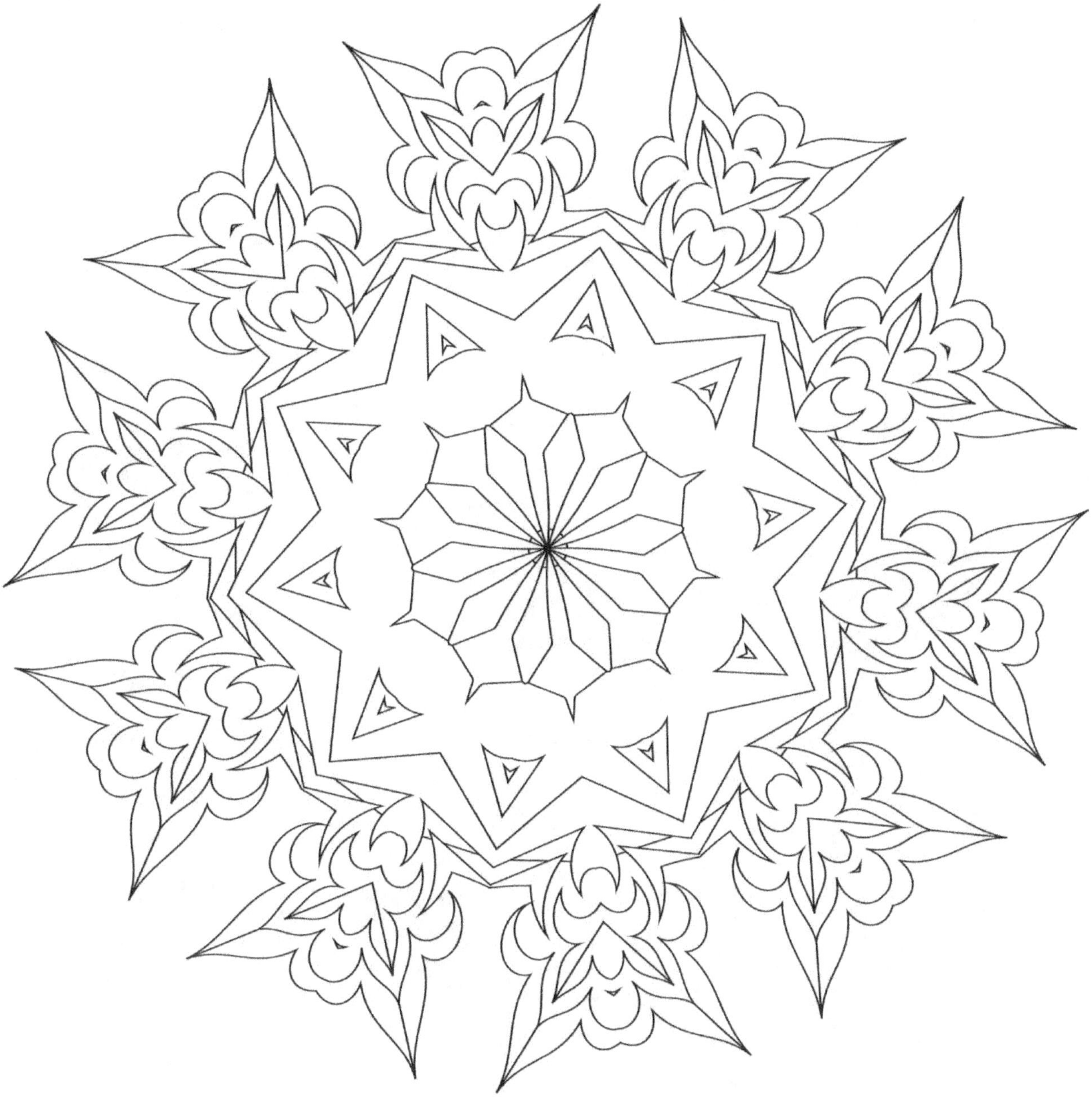

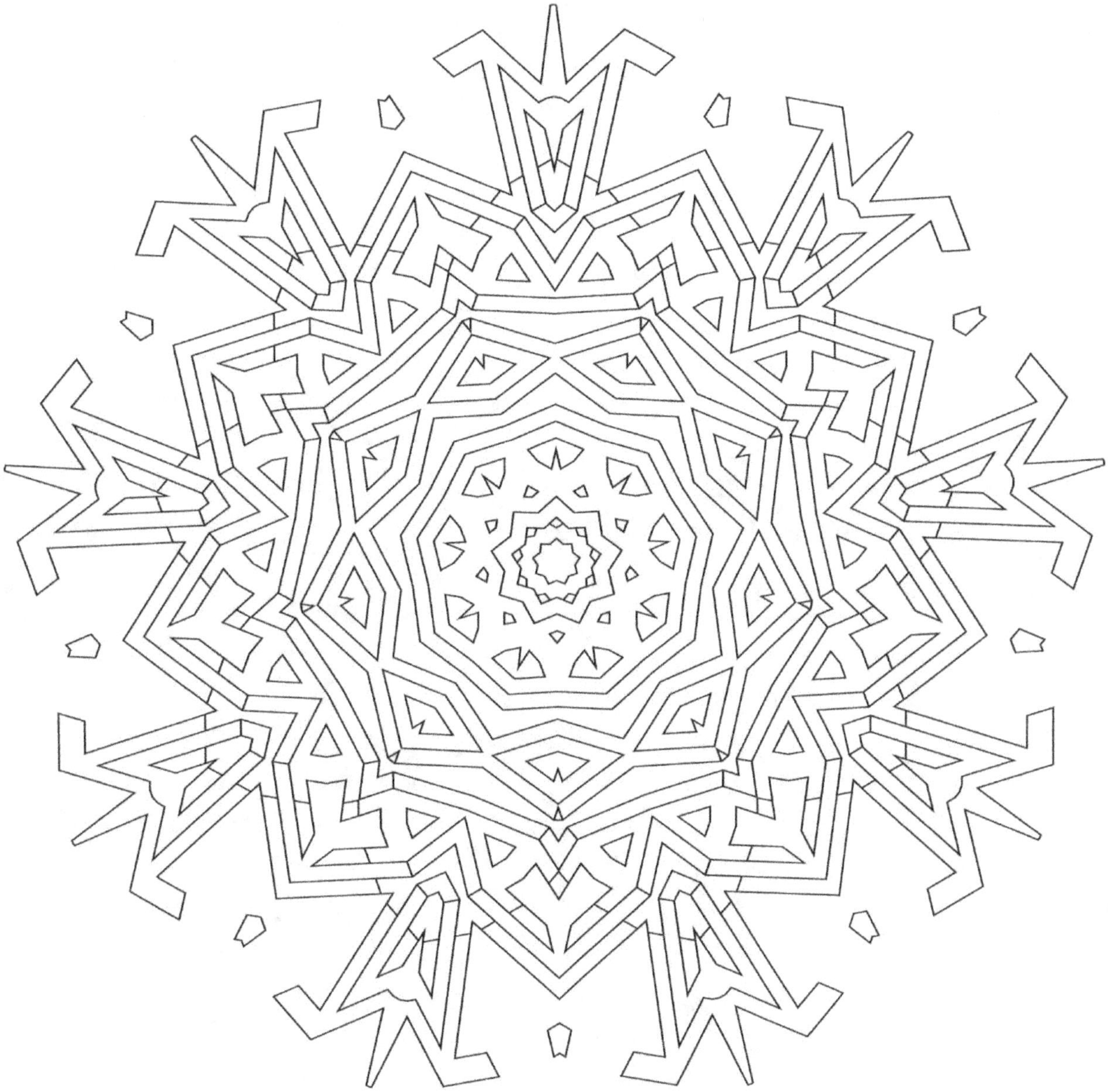

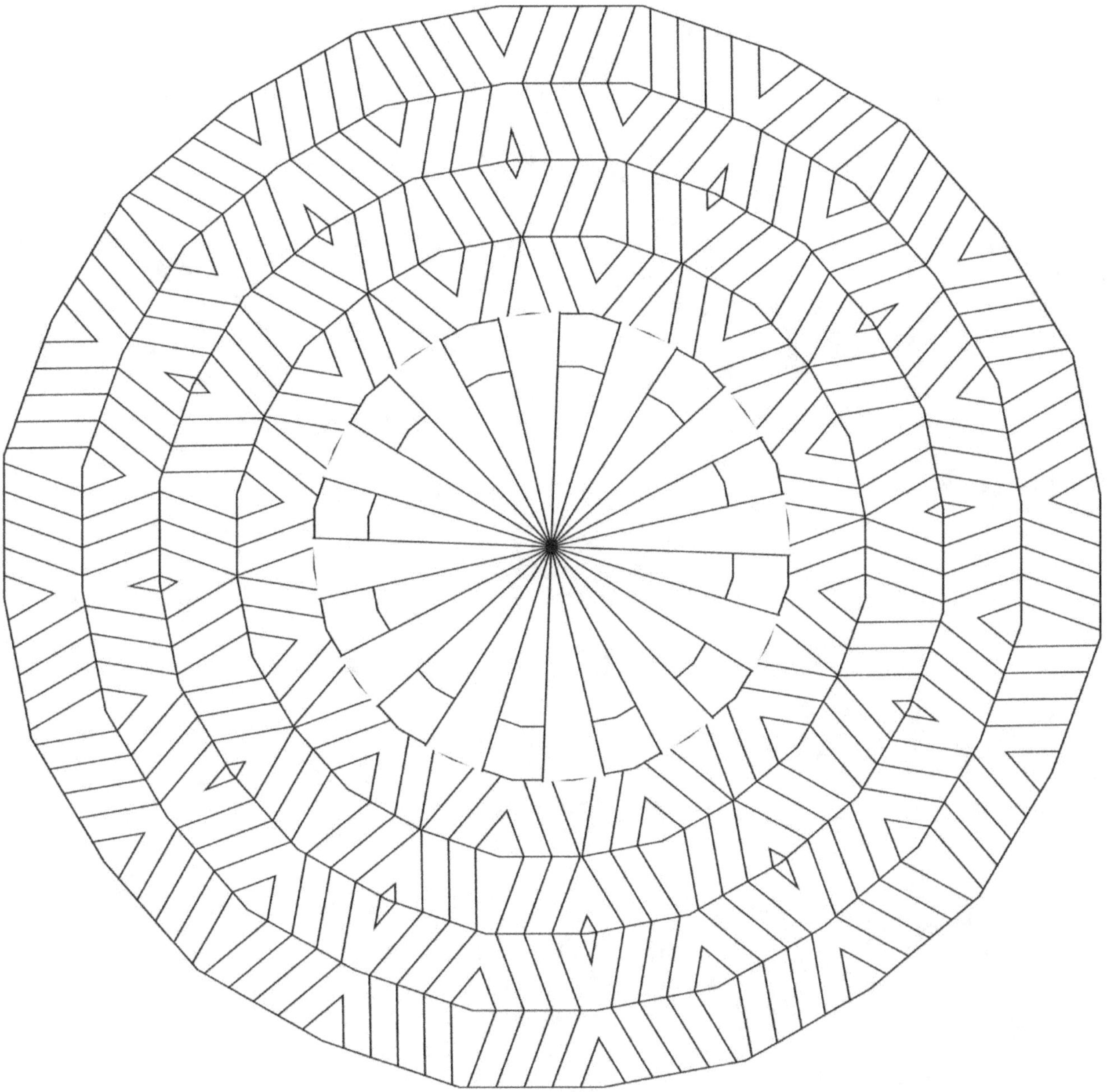

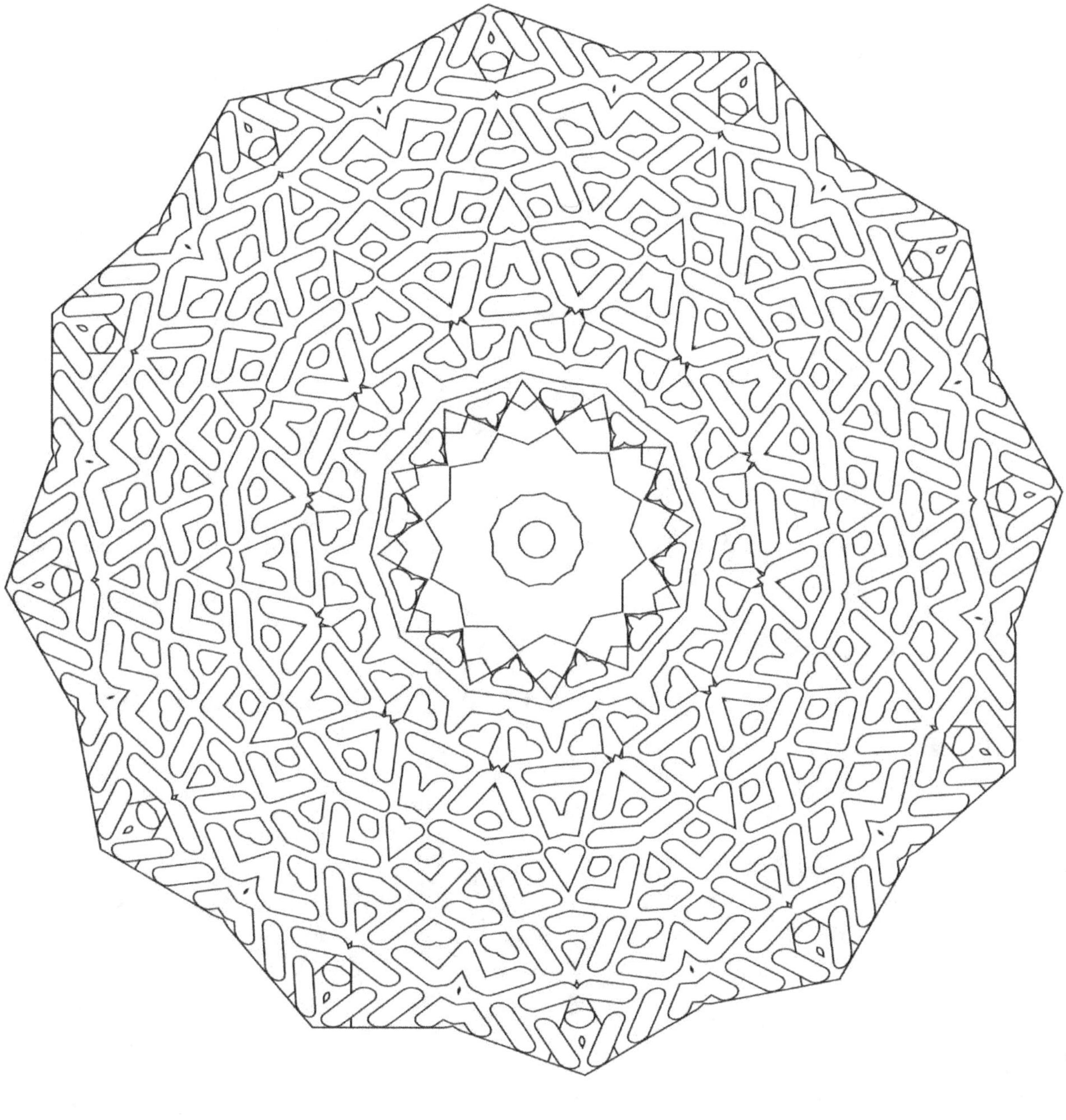

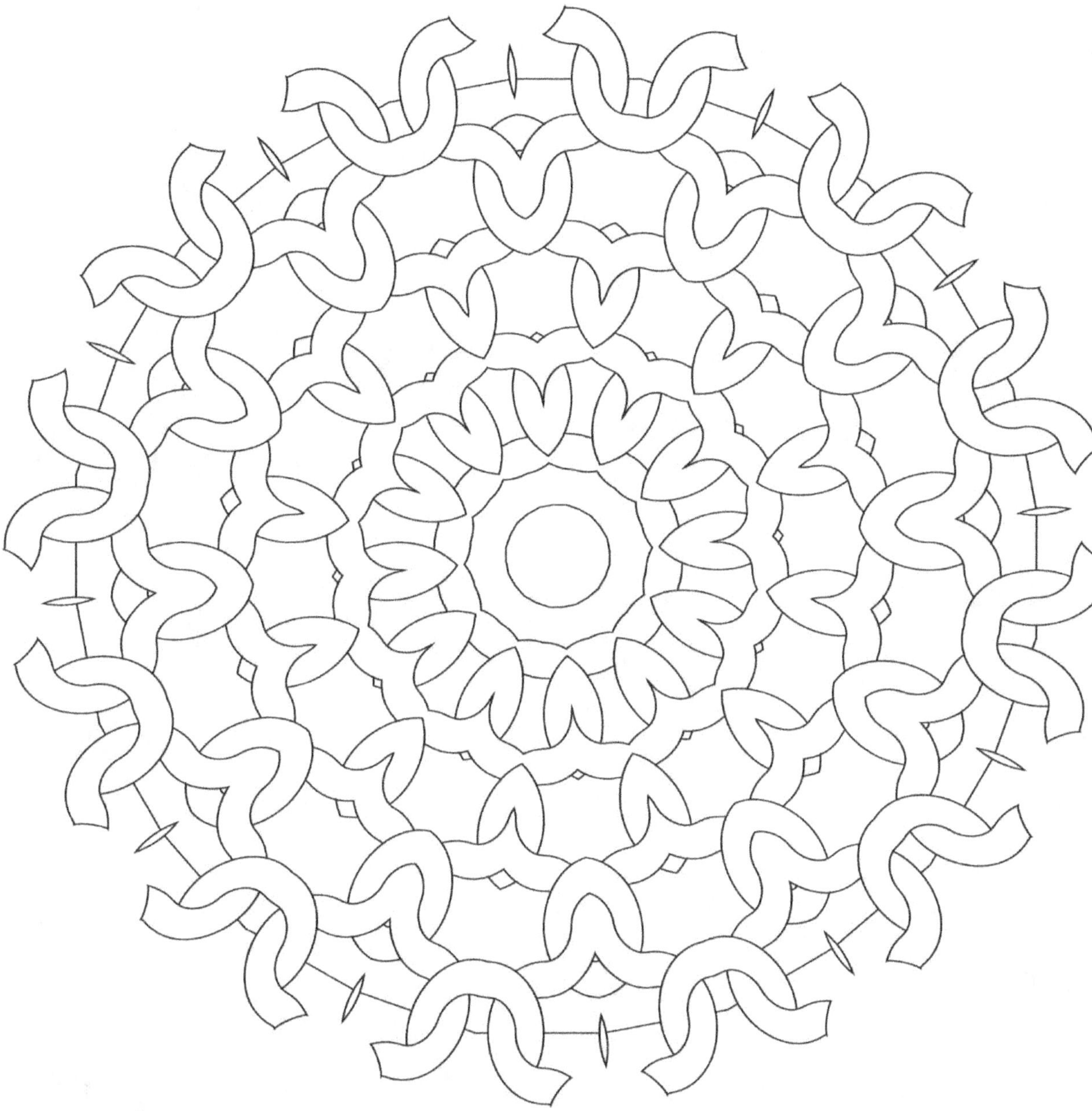

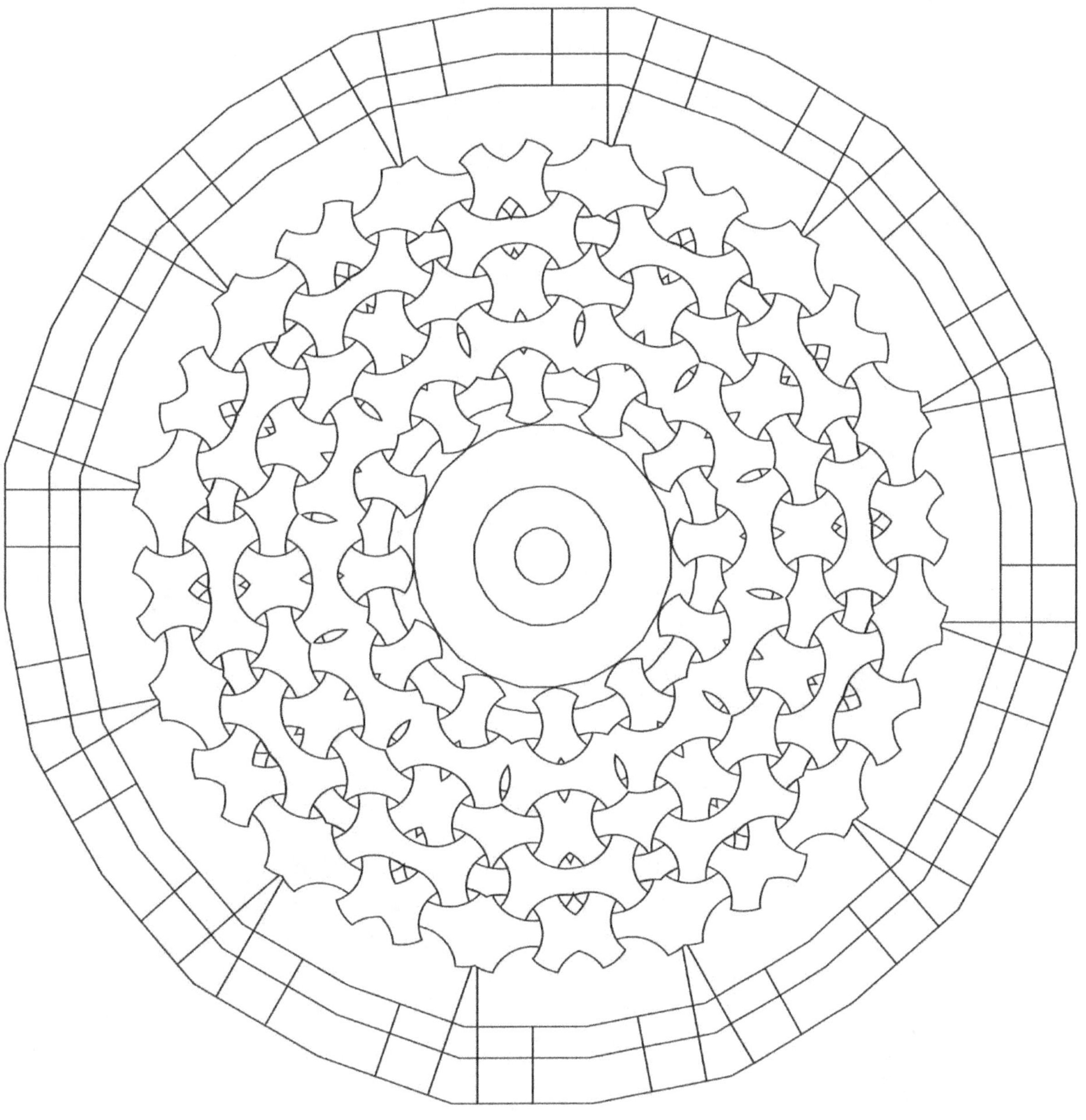

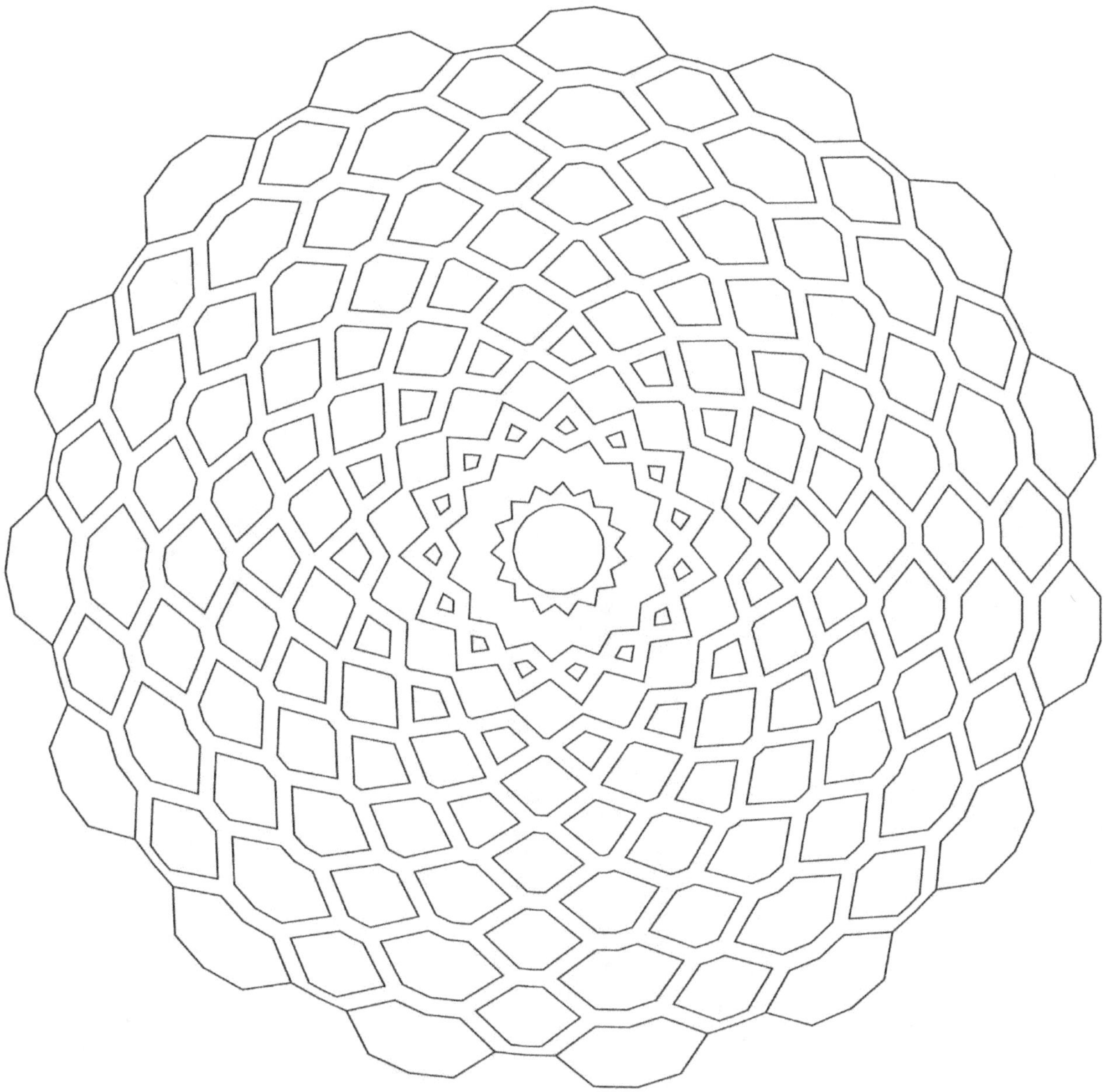

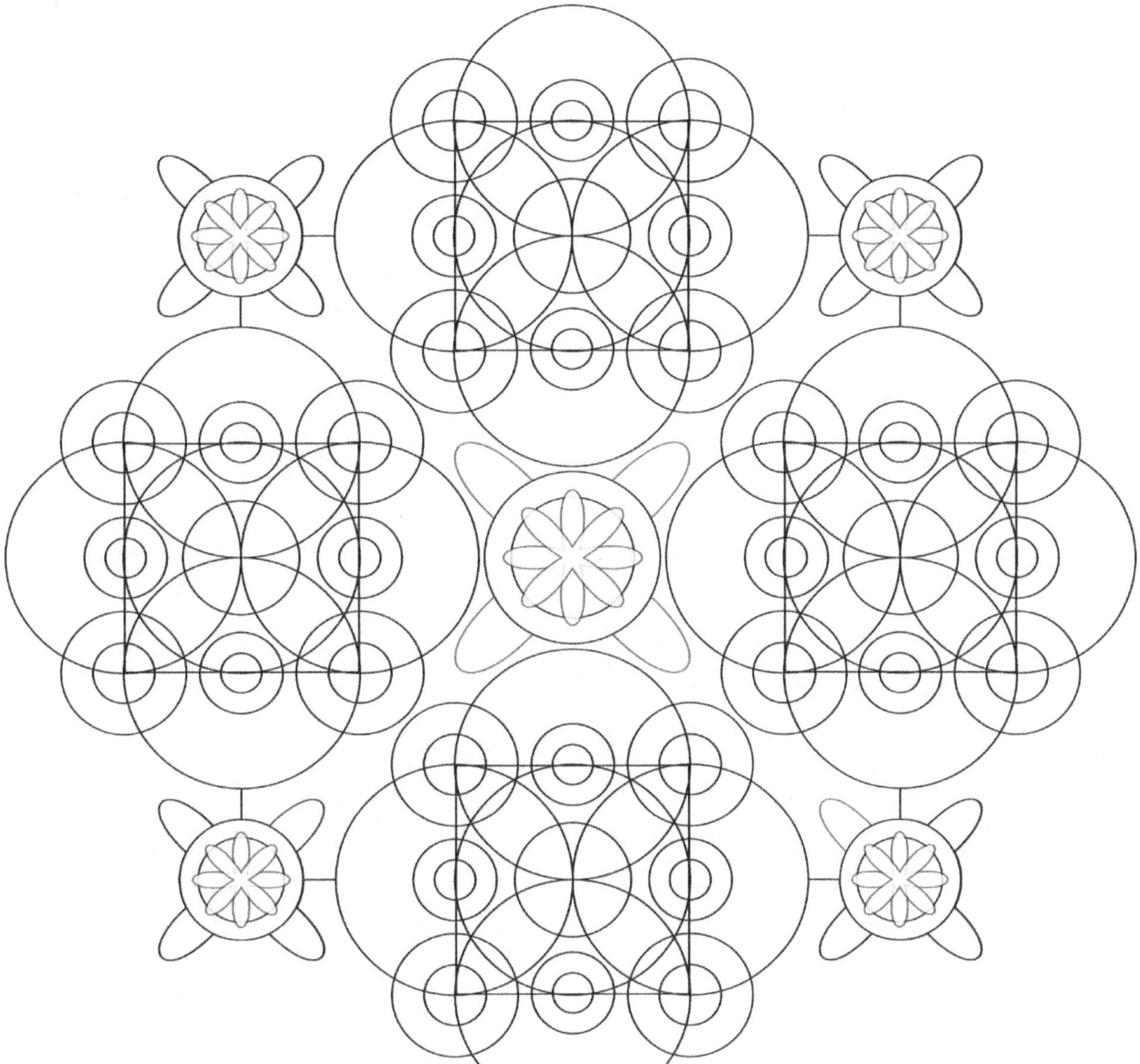

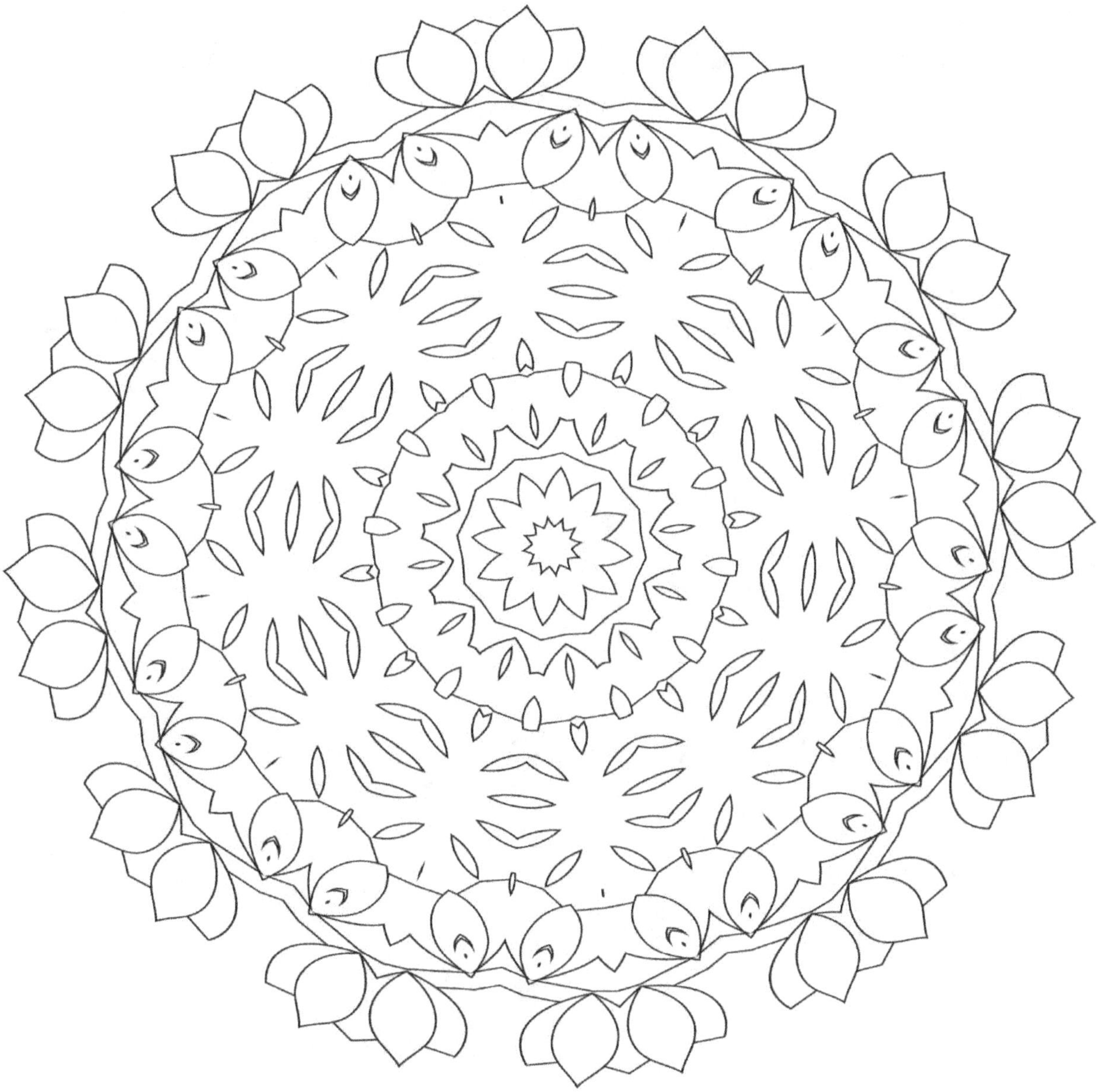

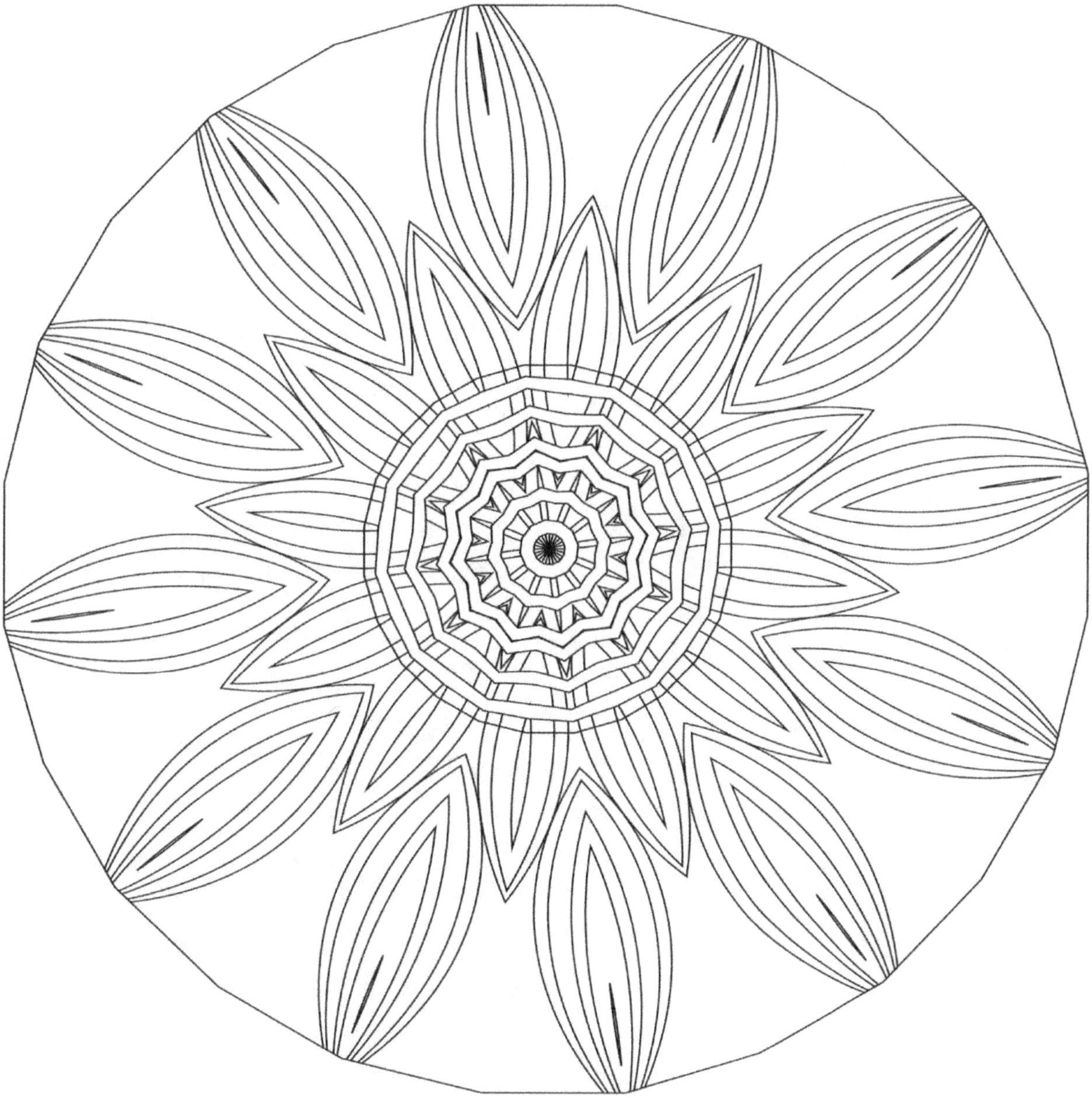

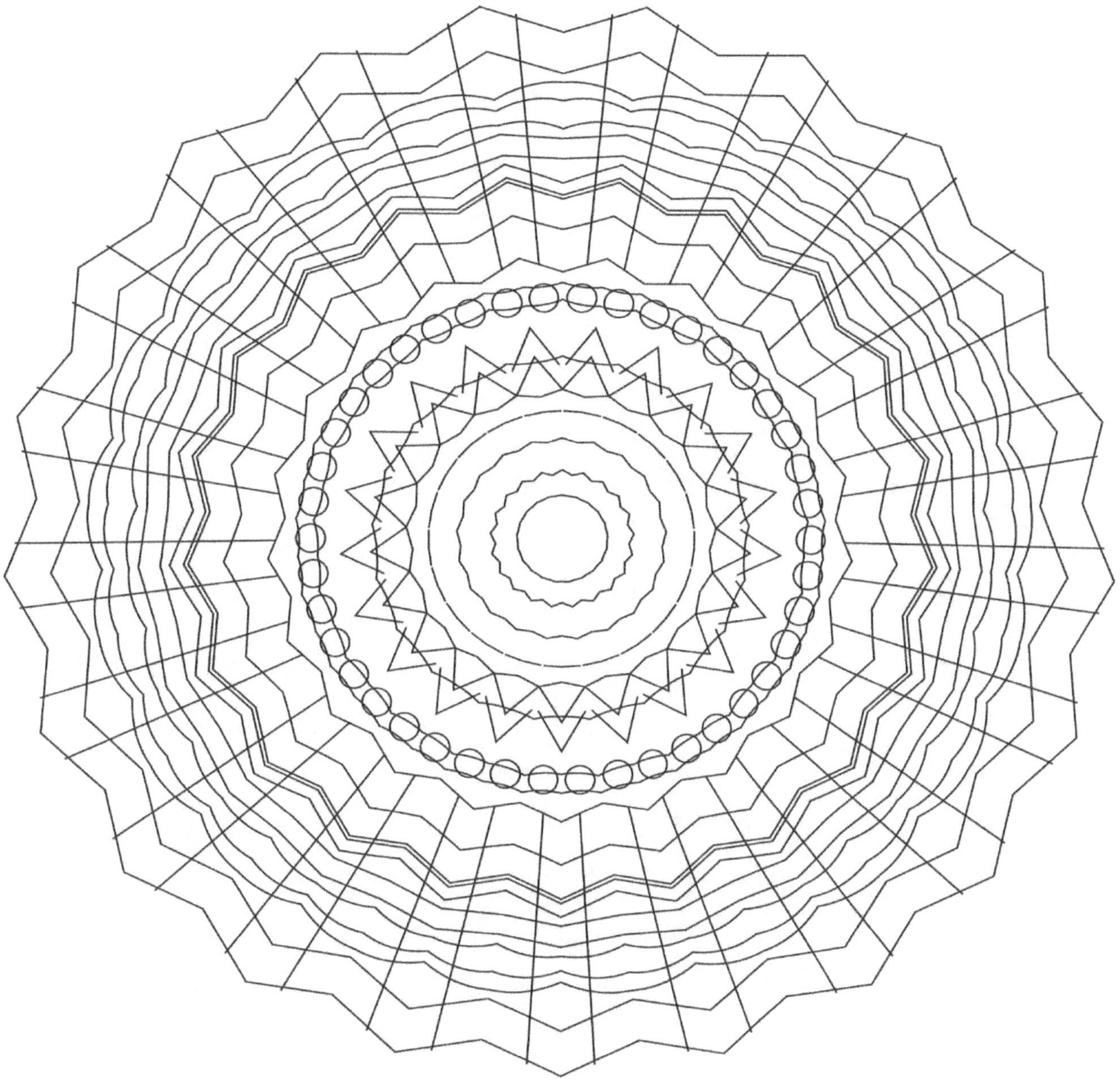

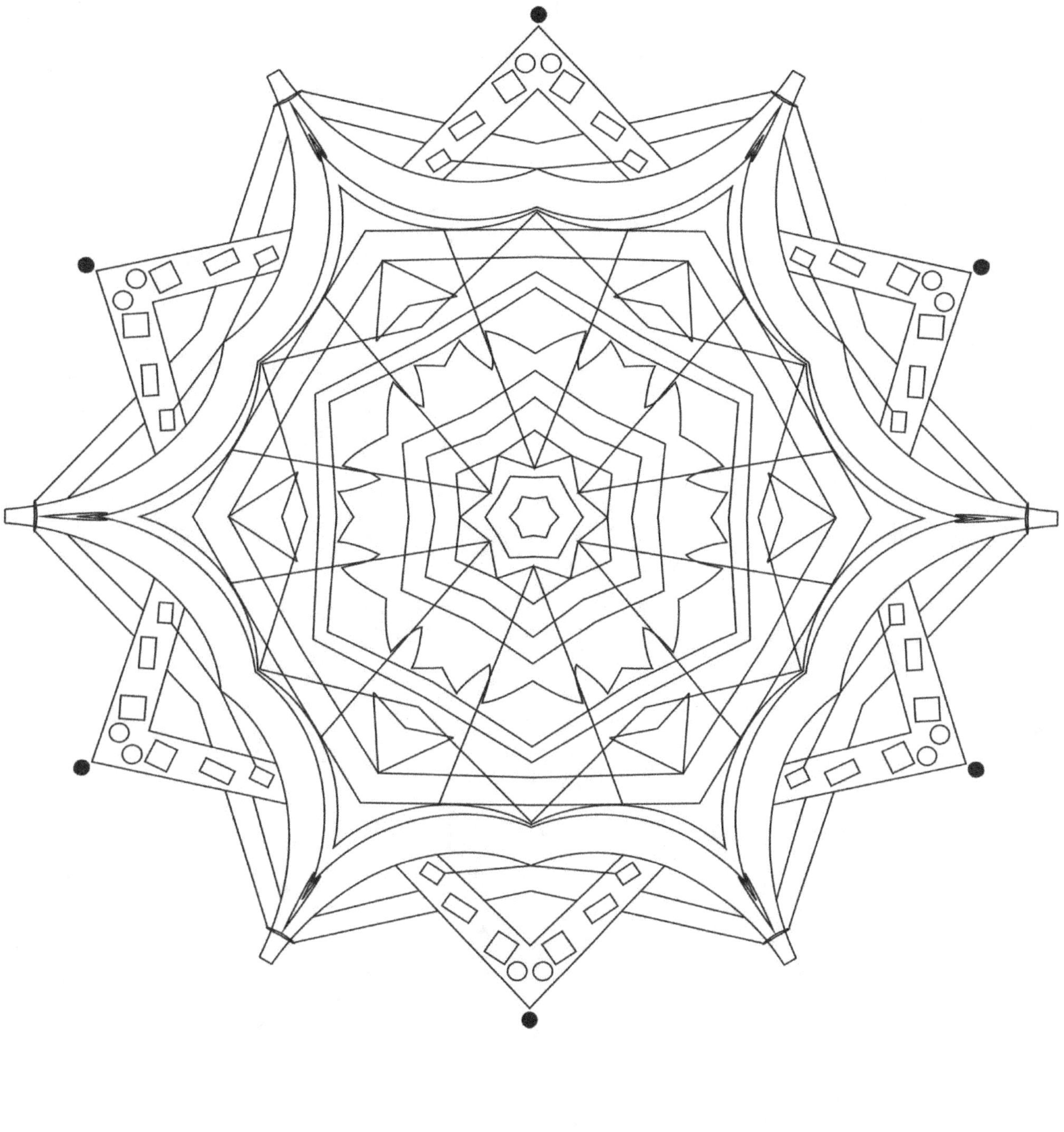

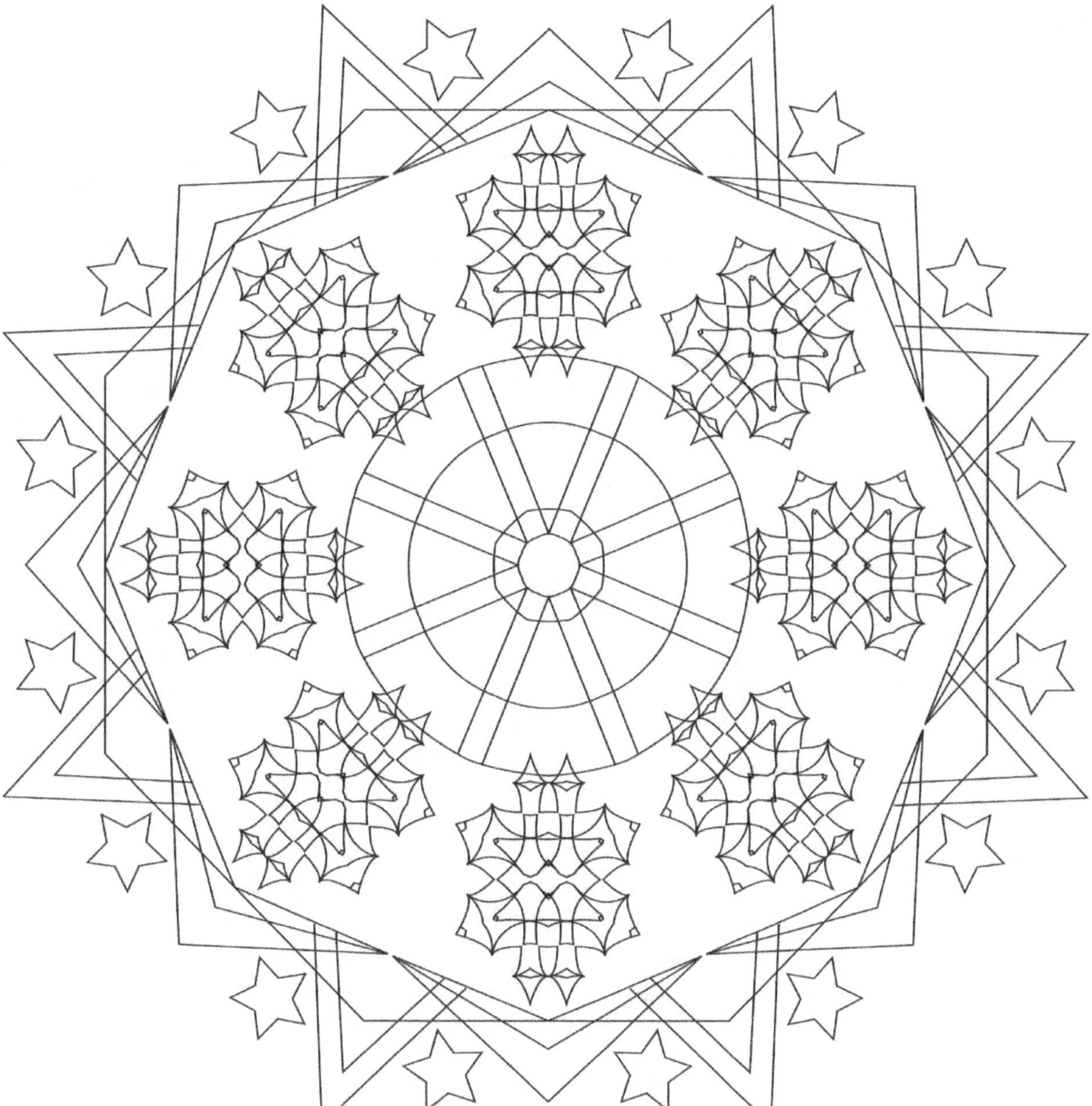

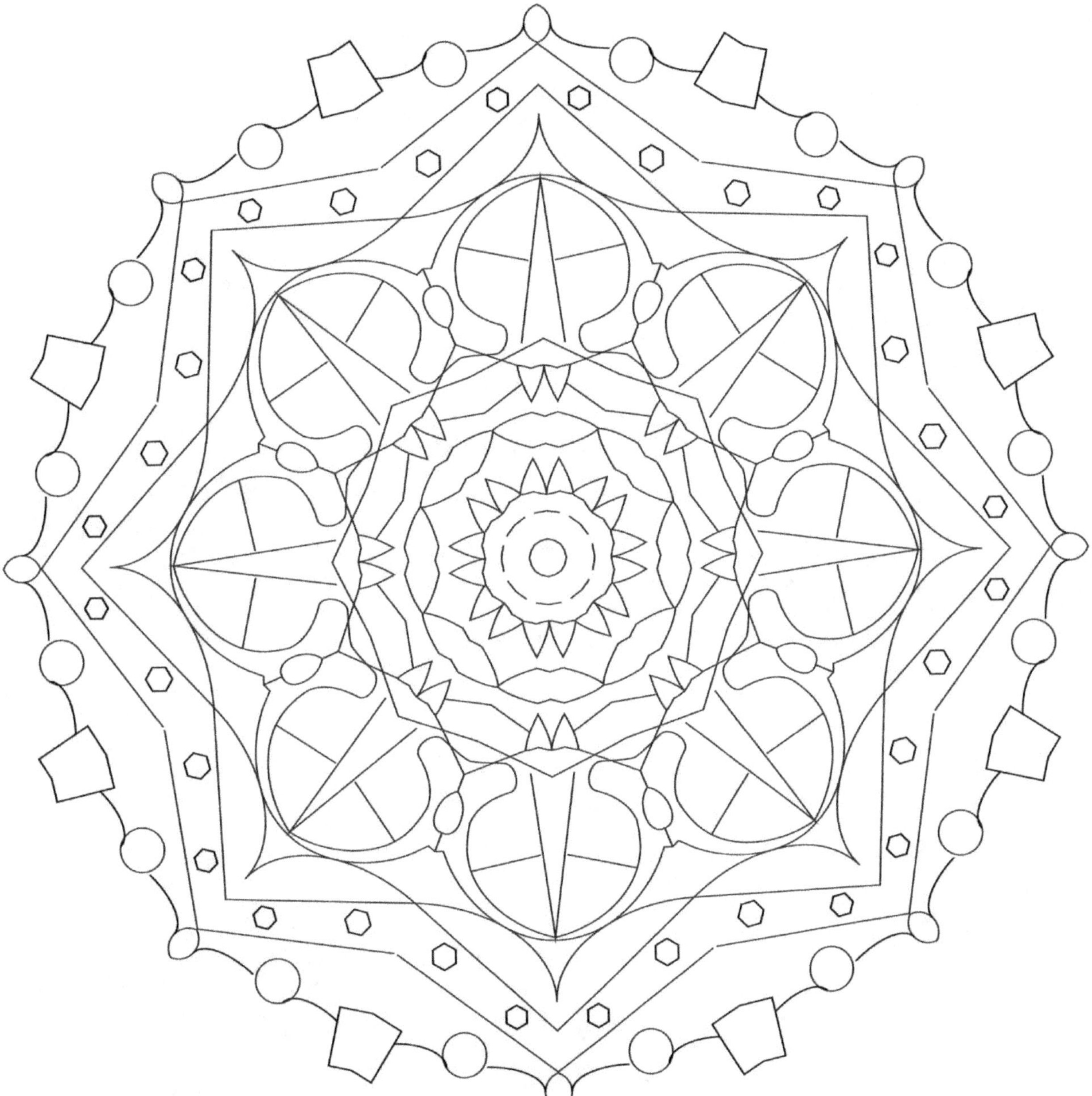

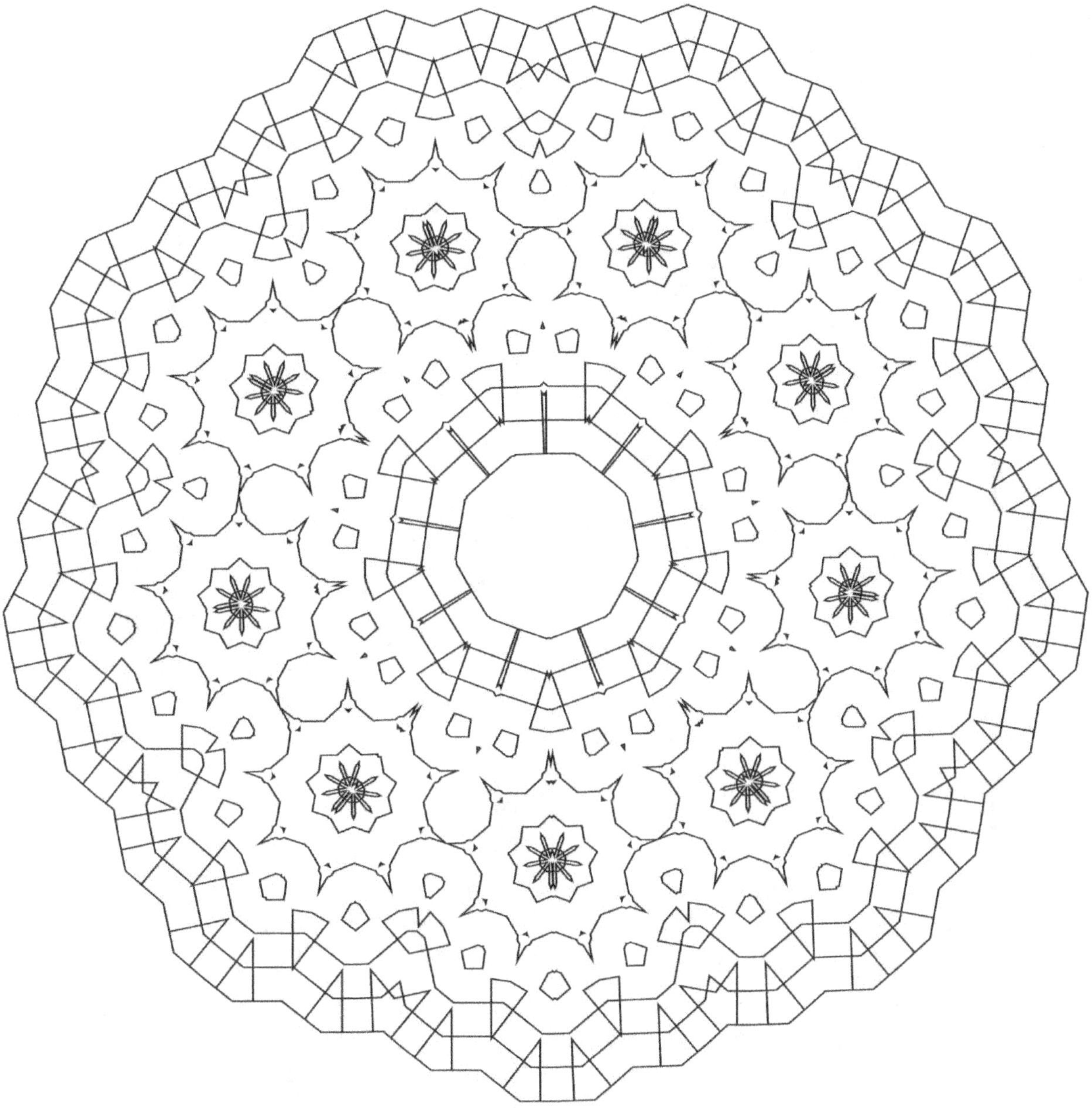

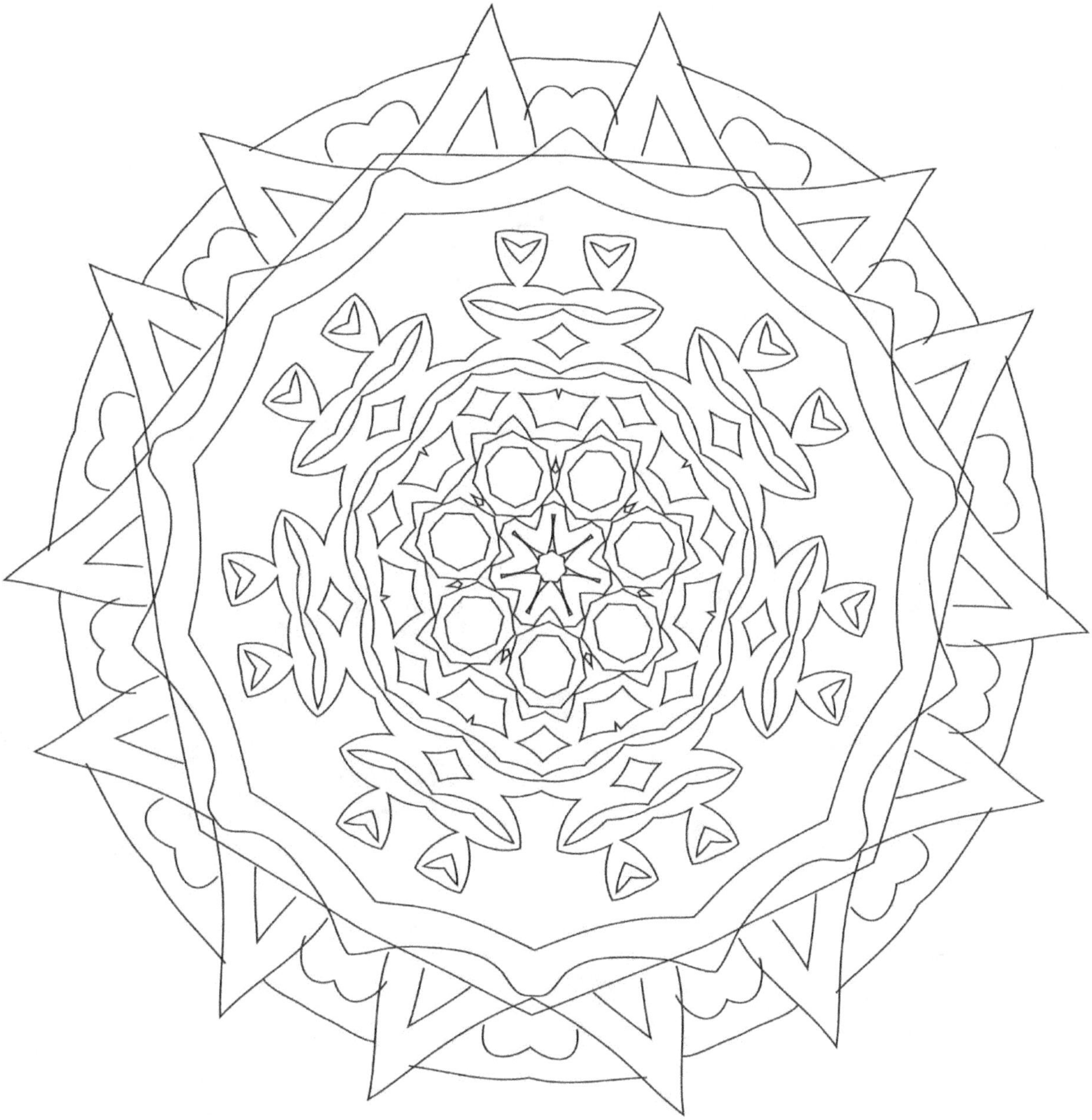

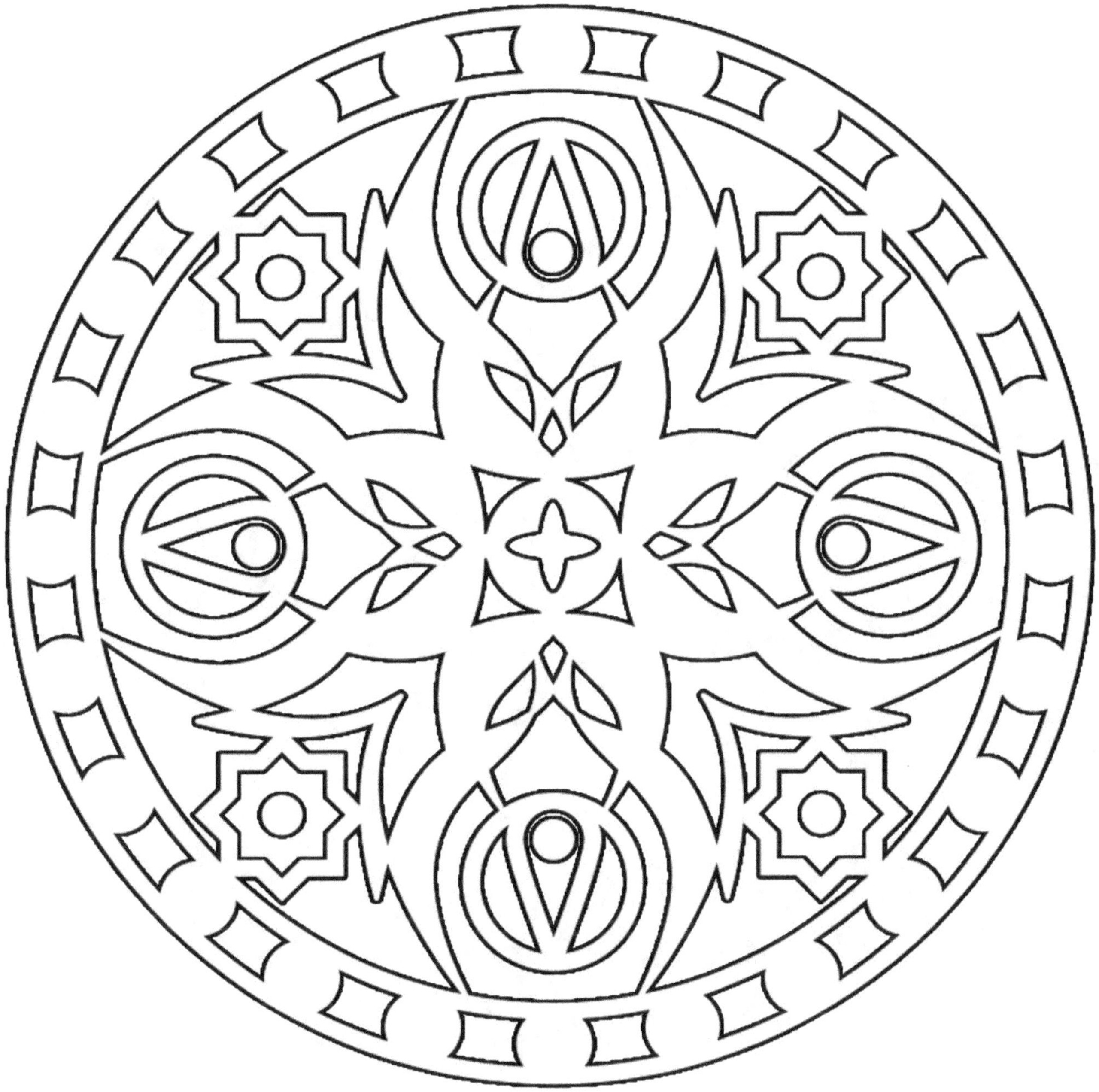

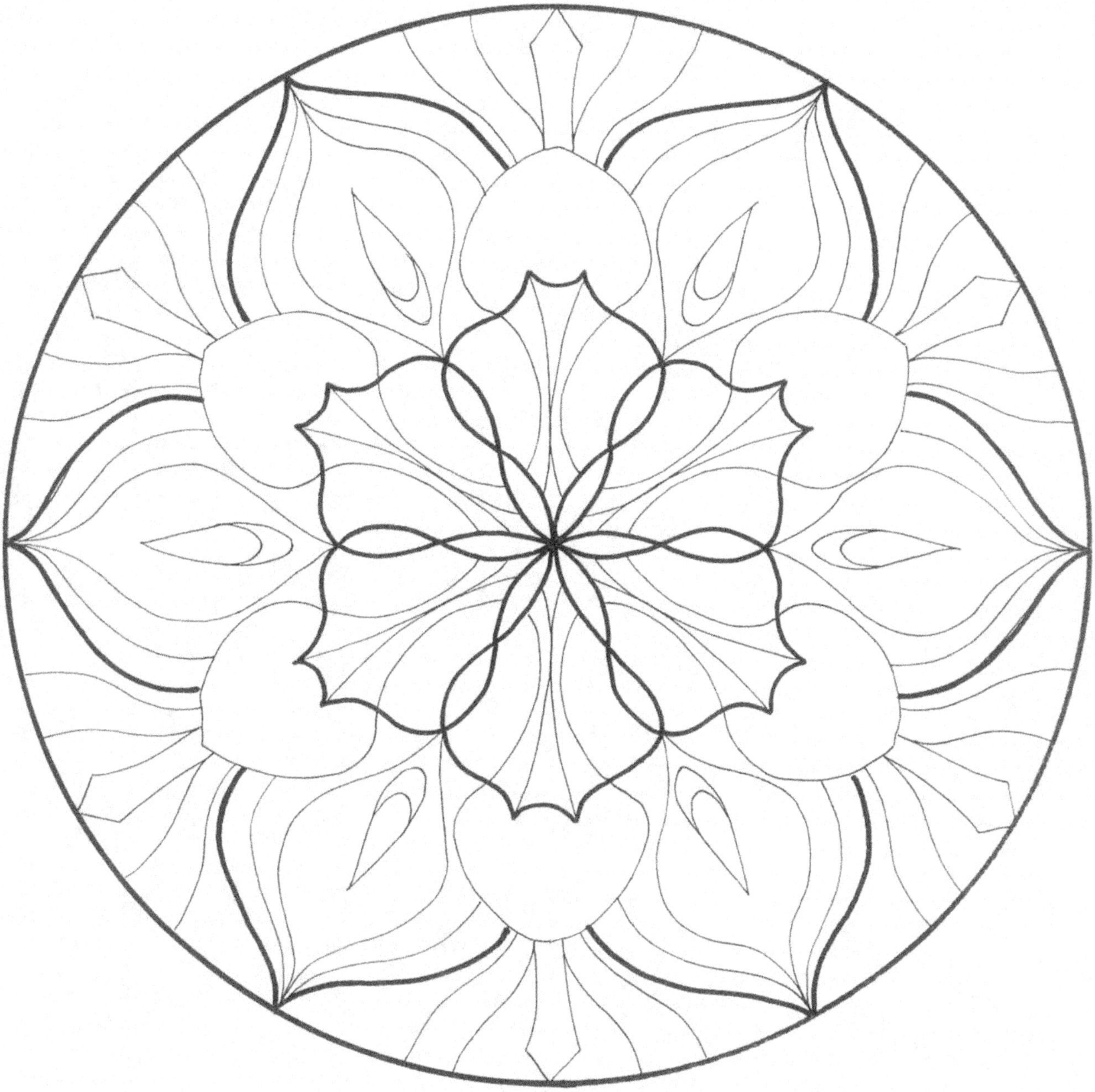

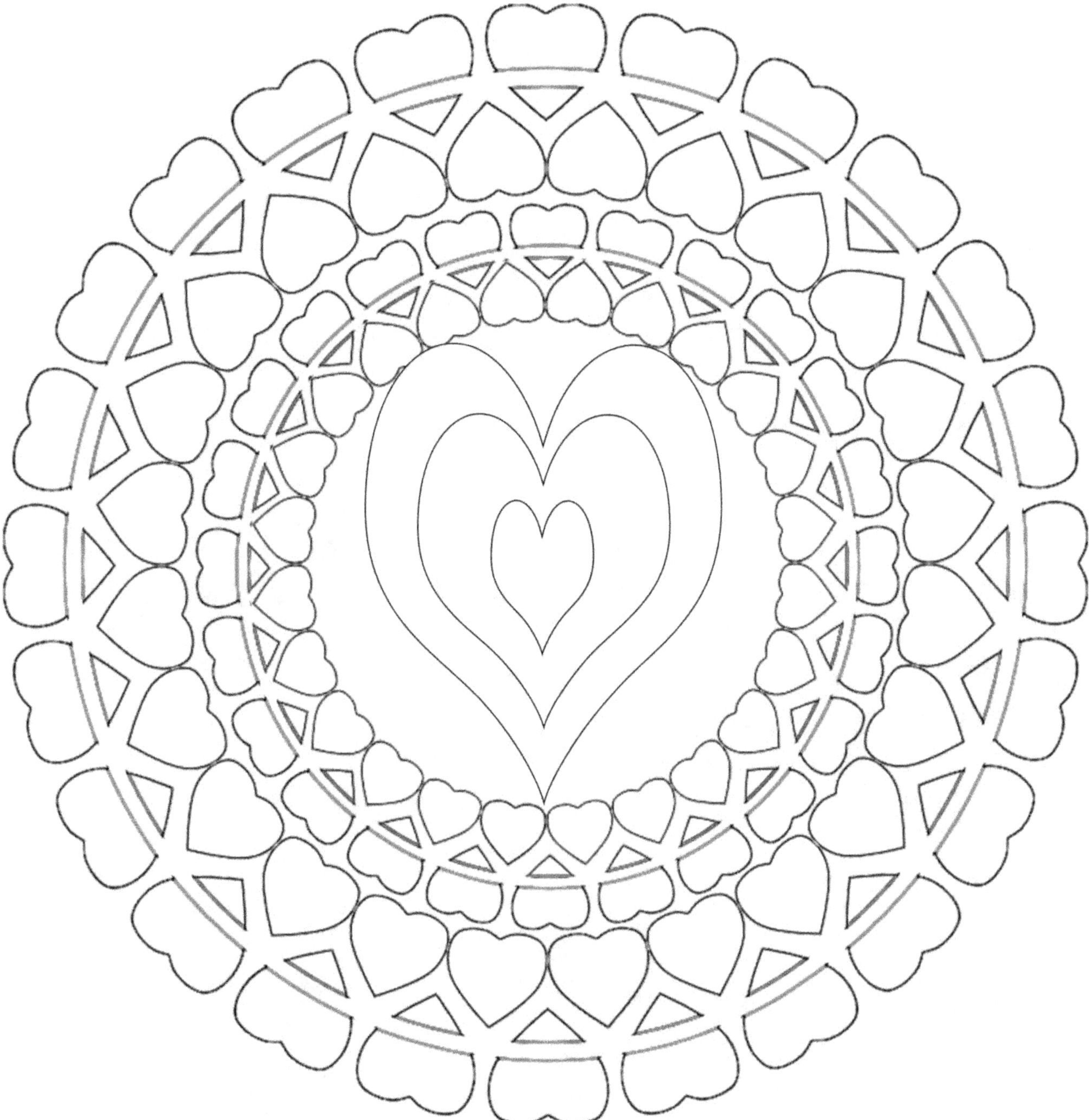

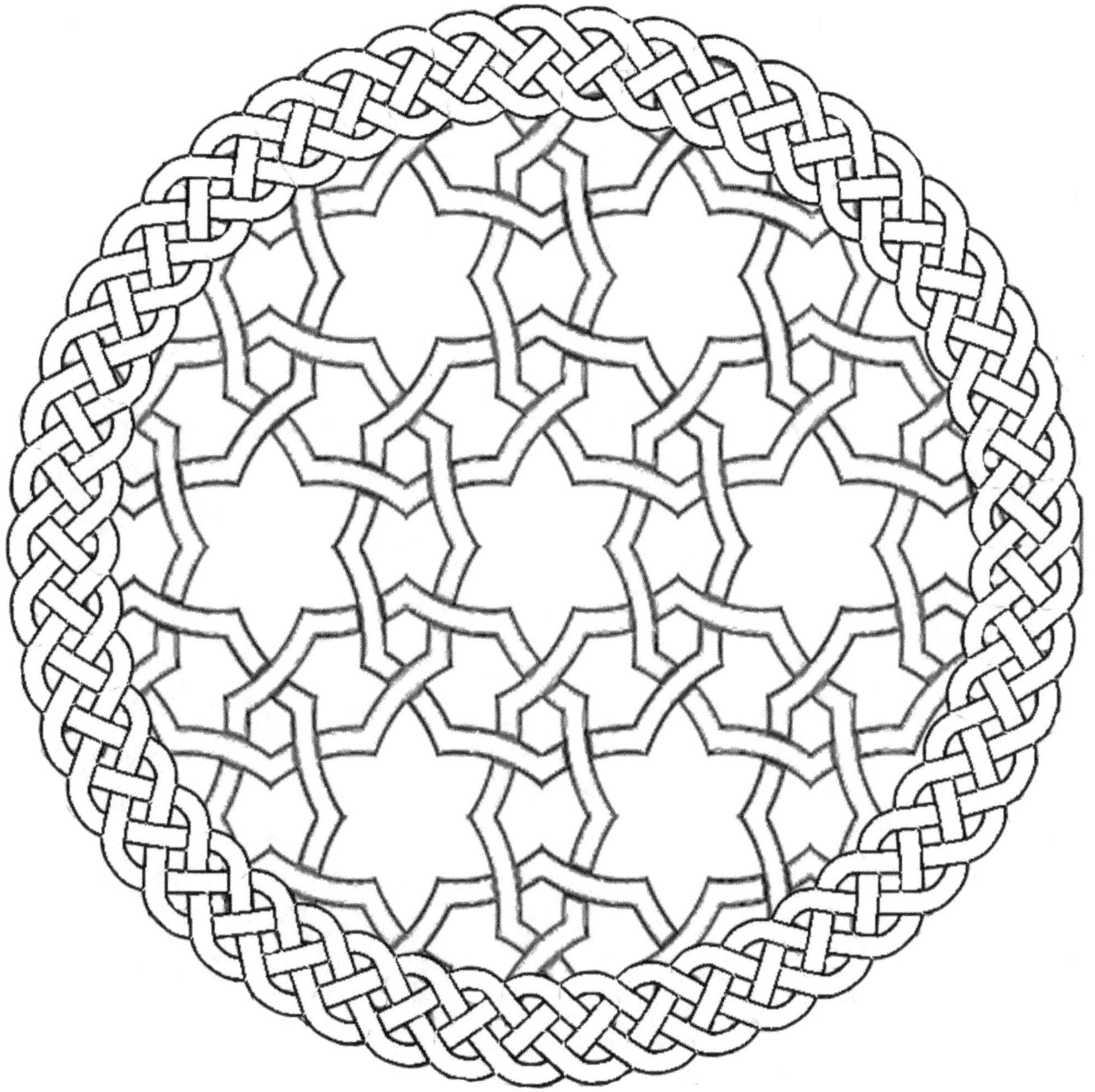

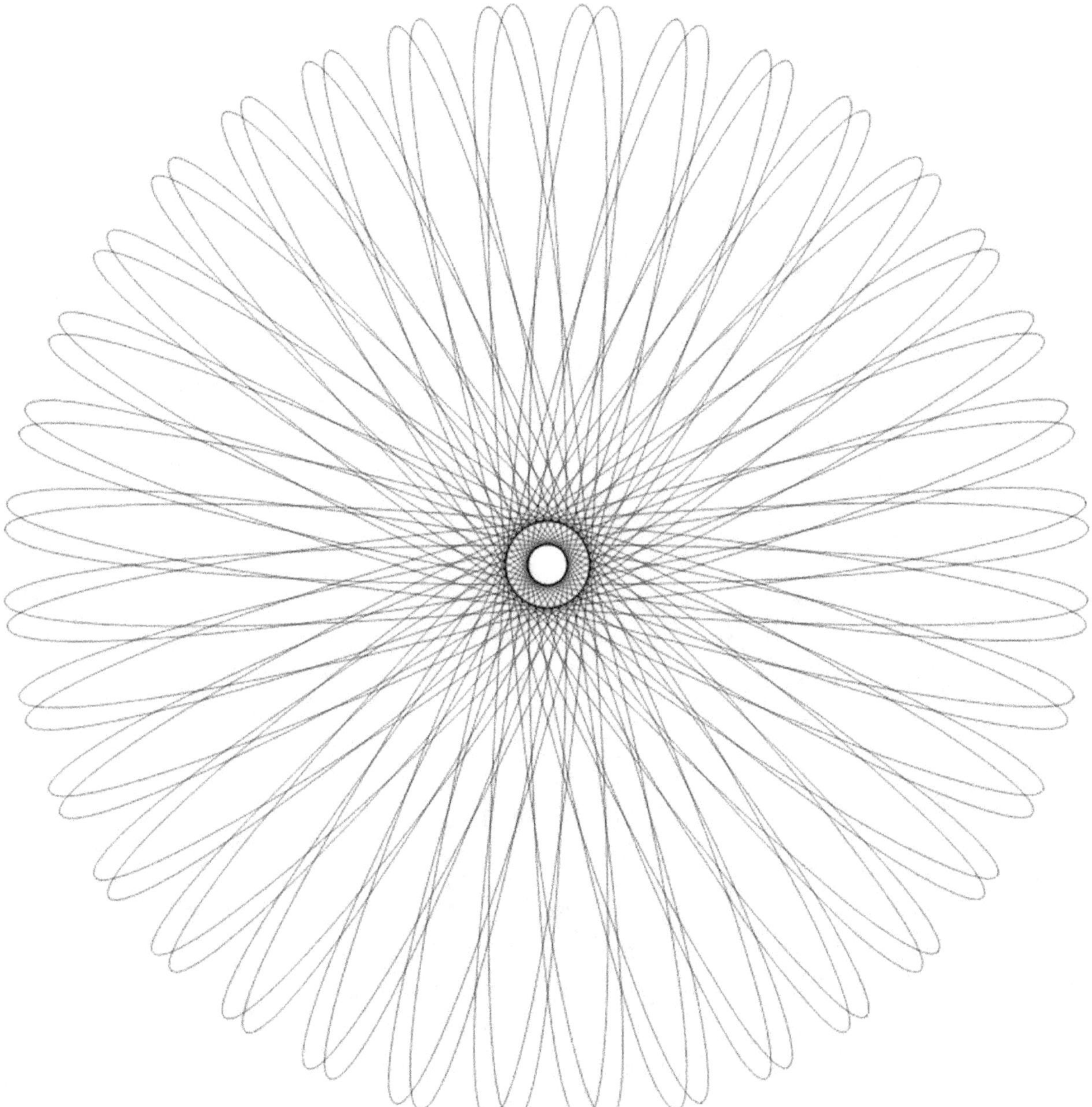

www.ingramcontent.com/pod-product-compliance
Lightning Source LLC
Chambersburg PA
CBHW081605170526
45166CB00009B/2828
* 9 7 8 1 5 1 9 4 8 9 7 5 3 *